At the Mercy of Kings

Everyone loves a good story and Linda Finlayson is a very, very good story-teller. As you read **At the Mercy of Kings** you'll discover what it feels like to be brought up in an English royal palace and then to be sent away from home aged just nine because your father didn't please the king. You'll imagine yourself in young Lady Mary's fine clothes for they are described so well. Then you'll feel sad when you read of her, aged just 15, being married to a cousin she'd newly met – and didn't like! And you may well feel sea-sick when you travel with Mary on her voyage across the English Channel to her new home in Holland where her husband was king. Linda Finlayson doesn't give away secrets till she really needs to. Does Mary grow to love King William? Do they have several little princes and princesses? You'll have to read the book to find out. After eleven years in Holland, William and Mary are called to be King and Queen of England and a whole new adventure began. There is danger and adventure; there is laughter and sadness in the life of Mary of Orange, who lived from 1662 to 1694. **At the Mercy of Kings** is the story of a young woman who put her faith in God and found that he kept all his promises even when her world turned upside down.

Irene Howat, Award-winning author

At the Mercy of Kings

Mary of Orange

Linda Finlayson

CF4·K

For Lauren,
who wanted to read the rest of the story

10 9 8 7 6 5 4 3 2 1
© Copyright 2012 Linda Finlayson
ISBN: 978-1-84550-818-0

Published by Christian Focus Publications
Geanies House, Fearn, Ross-shire,
IV20 1TW, Scotland, UK.
www.christianfocus.com
email: info@christianfocus.com
Cover design by Daniel van Straaten
Cover illustration by Brent Donoho
Inside illustrations by Jeff Anderson
Printed and bound by Nørhaven, Denmark

Scripture quotations are from The Holy Bible, *English
Standard Version*, copyright © 2001 by Crossway Bibles, a
division of Good News Publishers. Used by permission.
All rights reserved.

Contents

Taken Away

(1671-72)

Nine-year-old Mary and her six-year-old sister, Anne, stood still as Mrs Langford tied the ribbons on their cloaks and pulled up their hoods with more force than necessary. The girls exchanged fearful glances. Anne's little hand crept out of the fine woollen folds of her cloak and found Mary's. Together they stood back as their nurse heaved her short plump frame upward and resumed giving sharp orders to the ladies of the royal household.

'Make sure those boxes and trunks are well secured. Bessie, have you packed all the gowns and stockings? Mrs Leigh, stop dawdling and check the bedchamber for all the linens. Really, Mrs Walshingham, this is no time for tears.'

Mrs Langford, or Mam as the children called her, stood with hands on hips supervising like an army captain. Mary knew Mam wasn't angry with them, but they didn't want to get caught in the crossfire. The middle-aged woman had strong opinions and wasn't above voicing them even to her betters.

All at once Mary and Anne were herded out of the door of the royal nursery apartments and through the corridors of St James's Palace with Mrs Langford at their head. The parade of people, boxes and trunks went down the wide staircase, through the entry hall and out across the park to the River Thames where the royal barge awaited them. Once more Mrs Langford barked out orders, until all were stowed aboard. Mary and Anne, as the daughters of the Duke of York, were seated on the cushioned bench under a brightly decorated canopy at the back of the long barge. From there they could watch the eight rowers as they began to move their oars back and forth in a steady rhythm to propel the vessel around the twists and turns of the wide river.

Mary, eager to calm her sister's fears, whispered, 'It will be all right, Anne, you'll see.' But would it? she silently wondered. What was so terrible about their father that his own brother, King Charles, would send them away from him?

Mary shielded her eyes from the afternoon sun that had peeked under the canopy, and watched as they left London behind. The scene slowly changed from buildings built on the river's edge to marshes and green fields beyond. Only a few weeks ago, Papa had promised that nothing would change, but he had been wrong.

Their father, the tall, elegantly dressed Duke of York, had come to the nursery apartments in St James's Palace to tell them at the end of March 1671 that their mother had died. 'She suffered much pain from her illness and it's as well she's gone,' he had said. Then he added, 'I won't be going to the funeral and I don't think you girls should either.' Turning to Mrs Langford, he continued, 'Just have them dress in black for a while. That should be sufficient.' Then he gave both Mary and Anne a warm hug.

Mary had tried to remember the mother she hardly knew, but all she could recall was an enormous woman laughing at a dinner table surrounded by courtiers. Mary had lived with her nurse since she was a baby where Mrs Langford, her Mam, cared for all the royal children. Mary didn't remember her mother ever coming to visit the nursery.

'Now you're not to worry,' Papa had said. 'Nothing will change.'

But things did change within a month. A messenger from King Charles arrived and Mam had seen him in the reception room. Then she marched angrily into their playroom muttering, 'Jumped up woman! Thinks she's important now that her husband has been appointed as royal house and grounds keeper to all the king's residences.'

Mary and Anne laid down their dolls and stood up respectfully while exchanging confused glances.

'We're moving to Richmond Palace, where the king has arranged for you to have a new governess. Lady Frances Villiers,' Mam announced. 'Fortunately, the king realises how necessary I am to you, so I will go too.' Then the hurried preparation began.

That was all they had been told, and Mary had been too afraid to ask for more. Now a week later

Mary still didn't understand why the king thought his nieces should live with the Villiers family.

'Mary,' Anne was pulling at Mary's sleeve, breaking into her thoughts. 'I want to go back,' Anne whispered. 'What if they're mean?'

'Don't be a goose, Anne,' Mary replied with more certainty than she felt. 'They won't be mean to us. We're the duke's children.' She reached over and hugged her little sister. 'But I do hope they will be nice,' she whispered softly.

As they rounded yet another bend in the river, Richmond Palace came into sight and Mary's heart began to thud with renewed anxiety. The red and brown stone palace rose majestically from the midst of a large park and formal gardens. The three-storied palace had many round and octagonal towers capped with pepper-pot domes and an equally large number of windows.

The barge bumped gently against the wooden platform built by the water's edge as one of the oarsmen scrambled out to tie the vessel in place. The hard knot in Mary's stomach seemed to tighten up even more as Mam rose unsteadily to her feet, and began to order everyone about as they prepared to disembark. Mary stood up too, her sea legs sure, and turned to take her sister's hand to help her out.

'I won't go,' six-year-old Anne announced, her hood thrown back and the breeze blowing her long brown hair about her head. 'I want to go home. Now!'

Mary recognised that stubborn look on her sister's plump little face. When Anne made up her mind about something, there was no changing it. But Mary was more interested in their new home, so she turned away and climbed out of the gently rocking barge. Then she noticed some people coming down the pathway.

'Look, Mam,' Mary called back over her shoulder. Behind her she could hear their nurse urging Anne to move, but to no avail. In the end, Mrs Langford followed Mary out of the barge in time to be greeted by Colonel and Lady Villiers.

'Lady Mary,' the older gentleman said, bowing to her. He was richly dressed in brown satin breeches, vest and overcoat trimmed with silver buttons. He then introduced himself and his wife, Lady Frances.

'I bid you welcome.'

Mary nervously pushed back the hood of her woollen cloak, allowing her chestnut brown hair to tumble out, and gave a curtsy. 'Thank you, Colonel,' she managed through suddenly dry lips.

Lady Frances, younger than her husband and wearing a soft green silk bodice and skirt, stepped past her husband and swept Mary up in a hug. 'Welcome, my dear. You must be tired and worried with this sudden move. Please know that I'm truly glad that you and your sister are joining our family.'

All at once Mary relaxed into her new governess's arms, the anxiety of the last few days melting away. Whatever the reason they were here, at least the king had sent them to a kind woman. Stepping back from the embrace, Lady Villiers said to Mary, 'Your sister seems a little overwhelmed with all of this. Would she like a hug too?'

'I think so, although she is awfully stubborn,' Mary warned.

The governess smiled. 'I have six daughters and I think I know a little about young girls' ways. Mrs Langford,' Lady Frances continued, 'please go with my husband and take Lady Mary and the rest up to the house. I will bring Lady Anne.'

Mam gave a slight incline of her head and replied coldly, 'Yes, my lady.' Then taking Mary firmly by the hand she all but pulled Mary along up the pathway. 'Uppity woman,' Mary heard her mutter.

Mary never knew how their governess persuaded Anne, but before long both were at the door of their new apartment in the south wing of the house. A subdued Anne handed her cloak to Bessie, and then followed Lady Frances, Mary and Mrs Langford into the small receiving room. They settled themselves on some ornate cane-back chairs.

The room contained an empty stone fireplace on one wall and the remainder of the walls were panelled and decorated with paintings. Several large windows let in the afternoon sun, making patterns on the wooden floor from the window panes. A number of doors led to the other rooms where the girls and their household would sleep.

'Again, let me welcome you to my family,' Lady Frances said with a smile. Mary found herself smiling back and then caught the look of disapproval on Mam's face. Mary froze, unsure as to how she should behave, not wanting to offend either Mam or Lady Frances.

Lady Frances continued, 'I'm not sure if you have been told why you are here, so let me explain. The king has allowed my family to live at Richmond House and take you into my household to make sure you are properly schooled in the things that young ladies need to know, and in your religion.' Mrs Langford shifted noisily in her chair, which Lady Frances ignored. 'My daughters are already being tutored and you will join them in their classes along with a few other young ladies that the king has chosen as your companions. As for your religious education, Dr Lake has been appointed as your chaplain and he will instruct you in the Protestant faith.' Again, Mam shifted, purposely rustling the folds of her black silk gown.

This time Lady Frances spoke to the nurse. 'Mrs Langford, you are only here because the king didn't wish to distress his nieces with too many changes all at once. However, I must make one thing very clear. You may not discuss your Catholic beliefs at any time with Lady Mary or Lady Anne. You know very well that the Duke of York has converted to the Catholic religion and that this is the reason for removing the girls from their father's care. The king will not allow any interference with his nieces' religion.'

Mary straightened in her chair, trying to sort it all out. Mam was Catholic and now her father was. Yet the king was Protestant and he wanted them to be also. Why did it matter? They all went to church to worship God. But Mary sensed this was not the time to ask. Mam looked very angry and Lady Frances very stern.

'Will you agree to this?' Lady Frances demanded.

'This is really too much.' Mrs Langford complained. 'I'm the royal nurse. Have I not always taken good care of Lady Mary and Lady Anne?'

Both Mary and Anne cringed as Lady Frances rose from her chair. 'Mrs Langford, the king has given me the authority to care for his nieces and their household. You will do as I say, or you will be dismissed. Now let that be an end to it.' Turning once more to Mary and Anne, Lady Frances' face softened. 'We will dine shortly and you can meet my daughters. Then we will assemble for evening prayer in the chapel. You are to come to me at any time you have need and I will always listen.' She gave each girl a kiss on the cheek and left the room.

All at once Mary felt very tired and wished she could go to bed, but she obediently went downstairs to dinner with Anne deliberately lagging behind. The rest of the day passed in a cloud of weariness. The six Villiers girls, ranging in age from six to sixteen, eyed Mary and Anne silently over their dinner of duck and chicken pies. Mary was too tired for conversation, so the girls talked among themselves as if she wasn't there at all. Afterward, Mary unintentionally dozed during the evening prayer service and remembered very little.

Falling into bed beside an already sleeping Anne, Mary failed to say goodnight to Mam or say her usual prayers. She didn't even take time to wonder if their father was missing them.

Dr Lake Explains

(1672)

Over the next year Mary did think about her father often and she wondered if he really missed her. She remembered the day a few years ago when he had taken her and Anne to a court feast and danced with them as if they were grown-up ladies. All the courtiers had clapped and admired them. Mary had dreamed about doing that again, but it never happened. Although Papa did visit them in the royal nursery as often as he could, he was usually occupied with overseeing the Royal Navy.

Life at Richmond Palace was busy. Mary's and Anne's days were filled with lessons on reading, writing, dancing, drawing, music and learning French. Mary was especially good at dancing and languages. And she loved having so many new friends after living so quietly in the royal nursery. But Mary didn't like all of the girls. Betty was the oldest Villiers girl. At sixteen Betty thought herself very superior and Mary found her sharp-tongued and critical. And it didn't help that Betty's answers in class were almost always right. The other girls were great fun, especially Anne Villiers, who was Mary's age, and Frances Apsley, a gentle, older girl. Together the three played in the palace corridors, read romantic plays in the gardens, and wrote secret letters to each other. All of this helped Mary feel at home at Richmond, even though she still missed her father and her life in London.

But the whole matter of religion still bothered Mary. Every day she attended her catechism classes with Dr Lake, a kindly man who looked more like a soldier than a minister. Together the girls learned their questions and answers, memorised the Ten Commandments and the Lord's Prayer. Dr Lake also took time to explain what each answer or portion of scripture meant, so that Mary began to understand more and more about God and his Word, the Bible. Even so, Mary still wondered why it mattered so much that she had to be a Protestant and why it was so wrong for her father to be a Catholic.

One day, she went to her weekly visit with Lady Frances in her bedchamber. Her governess interviewed all the girls in her care every week. She reviewed their lessons with them, noting their successes and sometimes chiding them for any careless or foolish behaviour. Mary usually enjoyed these visits because Lady Frances also served tea, an expensive new drink imported from India. Mary felt grown-up drinking from the hand-painted china set.

'Come in, my dear.' Lady Frances welcomed her into her large bedchamber to sit on some yellow cushioned chairs by the fireplace. A small table had been set with dishes, a silver tea caddy that held the precious tea leaves, and a pot of hot water.

Mary settled herself, arranging her russet-coloured skirt in a ladylike fashion.

'I hear from Mr Gibson that your painting is improving,' Lady Frances began as she poured the hot water over the tea leaves. 'He thinks you may have a talent for painting miniatures after all. I suppose you just had a bad start?'

Mary kept her eyes on the dishes as she answered, 'Mr Gibson seems to think I should be much better than I am. He keeps telling me how well my grandmother drew when she was younger,' Mary complained. Then she looked up to see a look of disapproval on her governess's face. 'But I will try harder, and I do like painting,' she finished, trying to please.

'Of course you will,' Lady Frances replied. 'You have done well to adjust to our household,' she said as she handed Mary some tea. Then she changed the subject. 'Lady Mary, do you realise how important your religious education is? Are you listening closely to Dr Lake and learning your catechism?' Lady Frances studied Mary's face closely as she spoke.

Puzzled, Mary nodded. Was Dr Lake not pleased with her either?

'The king is most anxious that you learn the tenets of the Protestant faith, for one day you may be queen.'

Mary was horrified. 'But I don't want to be queen,' she suddenly burst out. She could feel tears begin to gather in her eyes. 'I'm just a girl. How can I be a queen? I don't know how!' and the tears overflowed.

Lady Frances swiftly set aside their dishes of cooling tea and gathered Mary onto her lap as if she were a very young child. Murmuring comforting noises, the governess held ten-year-old Mary against her until the tears subsided. Mary did not stir. She just wanted to go on being held and forget the frightening prospect of having to rule as queen.

With her cheek pressed against Mary's hair, Lady Frances began to speak softly, 'We are all called to serve God. My calling is to be a mother and a governess to the royal children. It is a great responsibility to see that each of you girls is properly taught so that you may go on to fulfil your calling. Your calling might be to inherit the throne of England after your father. So you must train for it now. Hush, now,' as Mary tried to protest while still holding her governess tight. 'You must accept what God has ordained for you. Now is the time for preparing and learning, especially about your faith.'

Her faith. That was the other troubling thing. Maybe now was the time to ask why it mattered that she be a Protestant and not a Catholic like her father. Loosening her grip, Mary sat up and suddenly slid awkwardly off her governess's satin gowned lap. Giggling at her ungraceful descent, Mary returned to her chair and then became serious once more. 'Why does it matter? About my faith?'

Lady Frances was quiet for a moment. 'I think you should talk to Dr Lake. He can better instruct you than I can. And you should ask him,' she continued hastily when she saw Mary's disappointed face. 'Dr Lake is your chaplain, your spiritual advisor. He is a wise man of God and he will answer your questions,' Lady Frances assured her.

The next morning, Mary knélt on the wooden kneeler in the chapel with the rest of the household and repeated the prayer of confession led by Dr Lake. After the prayer, they all stood to sing a Psalm and then sat to listen as Dr Lake read the scripture lesson for the day. His clear voice sounded throughout the chapel as he read from the first chapter of Joshua.

'Be strong and courageous. Do not be frightened, and do not be dismayed, for the Lord your God is with you wherever you go.' [1]

Could God make me courageous? Mary wondered as she thought about Lady Frances' advice to her yesterday. Could she ask Dr Lake about her father and his religion?

After the service ended Dr Lake came up to Mary.

'Lady Mary,' he said. 'I understand from Lady Frances that you have some questions for me. Shall we sit down here?' He motioned to some wooden chairs set up along the back wall of the chapel and he politely waited for Mary to seat herself first.

---

[1] Joshua 1:9

Dr Lake's face was full of kind interest as he began. 'You were taken away from your father's care last year just after your mother's death. You must have been very frightened then,' he said making his last statement sound like a question.

'Yes, I was,' Mary admitted. 'But not now. Lady Frances has been so kind.'

'She is a virtuous woman,' Dr Lake agreed. 'But you still have questions. About your father?' he probed.

Mary took a deep breath and plunged in. 'Why were we taken away? Why does it matter if he's Catholic? Why do I have to be Protestant? Why do I have to be queen? I don't want to be.'

The clergyman was quiet for a moment, studying Mary intently. While his face didn't look angry, Mary was sure she had said it all wrong and that he was disappointed in her. When he still didn't speak, Mary tried again. 'If my father is so wicked, why does the king allow him to stay at court? Why were we sent away?' she finished almost in a whisper.

Dr Lake's greying eyebrows shot up in surprise. 'Lady Mary, please be assured that you and your sister were sent away for your protection. Have you not said yourself, you are happy here? It's difficult to explain all the politics involved, but your father is very gifted in administration and he helps your uncle, the king, run the government. Not to criticise our good king, but he does need the help of your father in this regard.'

Mary felt a sudden relief to hear that Papa was not as bad as she thought. Maybe she would be allowed to see him again. But there was still the troubling matter of religion, and Mary could tell by the look of concentration on his face that Dr Lake was searching for words to explain the problem clearly.

'Your father, the Duke of York, has chosen to leave the true church and worship in an idolatrous one. It's bad enough that someone should do so in ignorance, but your father, who has been properly instructed, has deliberately turned his back on the truth.' He paused for a moment and Mary shifted nervously in her chair. Then he asked, 'Lady Mary, do you know who the pope is?'

'Um ... I don't know his name, but he's the head of the Catholic Church, is he not?' she replied hesitantly.

Dr Lake nodded, 'Yes,' and then he leaned forward and challenged her with, 'Should a man, who lives in Italy, have the authority to tell you and I, who live in England, what we may or may not believe about God?'

'No,' Mary replied without hesitation. 'Only God's Word tells us what we should believe.' Did Papa listen to the pope instead of God? Mary wondered. She picked at the lace around her sleeves as she thought. 'Does the pope tell all Catholics what they should do?'

Dr Lake sat up straight and folded his arms across his chest. 'The pope says he speaks for God, and all who don't listen to him will go to hell. The popes

23

of the past have corrupted the right teachings of Scripture. They say that Christ's death on the cross was not enough and that each time they celebrate the Mass, the communion bread and wine becomes Christ's body and blood, to be sacrificed again and again. This teaching is wrong, Lady Mary. There's more, but I think that is enough for just now. Your father has turned from the truth and serves a foreign pope instead of God. He thinks his salvation can only be earned by continual good works and hearing the Mass.'

Mary was horrified. 'He can't go to heaven if he doesn't trust in Christ. Has no one told him?'

Dr Lake sighed. 'Your father is a stubborn man. He will not hear the truth. That's why you had to be removed from his care. You might be queen one day. The people of England wish to worship God in truth and they need a queen who loves and serves God as they do.'

Even the thought of ruling England did not distract Mary from her concern for her father. Papa was deliberately imperilling his soul. Not only would she not see him much in this life, she would never see him in the life to come. Her thoughts churned away as she plucked even harder at her lacy sleeves.

'But what about Papa?' she asked her spiritual teacher.

'Pray for him. Only God can change his heart. Learn God's truth well, so that you may always be able to give an answer whenever you hear wrong doctrine taught. God has decreed how he is to be worshipped and served and no one may add or subtract from his Word.'

* * *

Mary prayed earnestly for her father after her long talk with Dr Lake. At first she was convinced that God would answer her right away, but as the year wore on she began to wonder if God was listening to her at all. She became discouraged and ceased to pray for him as often as she knew she should. Then one day in early autumn of 1672, a messenger arrived from the Duke of York summoning his daughters to London. Both Mary and Anne were excited and a little worried as they prepared for their journey up the River Thames. Lady Frances had refused to say what was so important that the King was allowing them to return to the court. Mam too was quiet, but she was smiling much more than Lady Frances since the message had been delivered.

A New Mother

(1673 – 1674)

The boat ride was wet and cold and eleven-year-old Mary pulled her red velvet cloak close around her while she and Anne huddled under the dripping canopy. Lady Frances and Mam sat under a smaller canopy, silent and staring straight ahead. The only sounds were the splashing of the oars and the call of the birds in the marshes. Mary was sure they were going to hear bad news and fear began to grip her insides.

As they were ushered into their old nursery apartments in St James's Palace, servants stood by ready to remove their wet cloaks and deal with their baggage. Lady Frances took charge, overriding Mam as she began to give instructions about what trunk went where in the series of rooms. Mam went grudgingly with the servants to supervise the unpacking. Just then the heavy oak door swung open and their father entered the room. The Duke of York's strong face was framed by a curly blonde wig that hung past his shoulders. He was dressed in silver and blue silk breeches and doublet with a billowing white shirt underneath.

'My daughters,' he greeted them, his arms wide to embrace them both.

Mary and Anne quickly curtsied and then threw themselves into his embrace. Laughing, the duke almost lost his balance. Righting himself, he returned their hugs and then stepped back to look at them.

'How you've both grown. You'll be young ladies soon. But not too soon I hope for I have brought you a new playmate.'

Mary and Anne exchanged puzzled looks. What was Papa talking about?

The duke waved his hand toward the open door where a lovely young woman with dark hair and pale skin stood. She was dressed in a deep purple silk bodice and wide overskirt that was pulled back on each side to reveal row upon row of silver lace cascaded down the front of the underskirt. But above the lace trimmed neckline the young woman's face was sad and apprehensive. Mary and Anne stared back, their mouths slightly open with surprise.

'Duchess Mary Beatrice, may I present my daughters, Lady Mary and Lady Anne. Daughters, your new mother,' the duke finished with a broad smile.

All three continued to stare at each other until finally Mary came to herself and performed a deep curtsy to the duchess. Anne quickly followed her example.

As they rose, the young duchess smiled at them and Mary realised that Mary Beatrice was not much older than herself.

'Oh, come now!' the duke said impatiently. 'She's your mother. Greet her with a kiss.'

Mary, feeling sympathy for the sad young woman, quickly ran to plant a kiss on her cheek.

'Welcome, Your Grace,' Mary said.

Mary Beatrice reached out and hugged Mary. 'Thank you,' she replied softly in Italian-accented English. And then she motioned Anne to come and receive a hug too.

The duke nodded with satisfaction. 'There now, we're one happy family.'

Behind them Lady Frances gave a discreet cough. The duke turned, his smile turning to a frown. 'Yes, what do you want? Can't you leave us in peace?'

Lady Frances' eyebrows rose in momentary surprise and then she appeared to collect herself and replied quietly, 'It is almost time for evening prayers. I must take Lady Mary and Lady Anne to the chapel.'

The duke swore at her in anger which made Lady Frances flinch, but she stood her ground. Mary gasped and would have cried out to her father if her new stepmother had not grasped her arm and squeezed it. Startled, Mary turned to see Mary Beatrice shaking her head and putting her finger to her lips.

'If there are any prayers to be said, they'll be said in my chapel where the true religion is practiced. Now leave us,' he ordered.

Reluctantly, Lady Frances curtsied and left the room.

Taking a deep breath to calm his temper, the duke turned to them and managed a smile. 'Let's go to supper,' he said as if the incident hadn't happened.

Dutifully Mary, Anne and Mary Beatrice followed the duke to his apartments where a private hot supper had been prepared. The reception room was warmed by a fire in a stone fireplace on one wall. A large, colourful tapestry hung on another wall and painted portraits on the other. Across from the fireplace was a large window to the outer part of the palace. Mary could hear noise on the streets below, but it was Anne who rushed over to the window to look out.

'Oh, what are those people doing with that straw person on a pole? Oh, dear! They're going to burn him in the big fire.' She looked back in the room with fear in her eyes.

'Come away from the window, Anne!' her father ordered. 'We want nothing to do with that rabble.'

'But why are they doing that?' Anne persisted.

'Because they are ignorant and foolish,' he replied, striding over to his daughter and leading her away from the window. 'Now, let's sit and enjoy our family meal.'

They were seated around the oak table in the centre of the room and the servants brought in a meal of eel pies, baked fish, and roasted pigeons along with quantities of cheese, apples and wine.

'There now, this is better,' the duke said as he pulled apart a pigeon with his hands. 'The duchess came all the way from Italy to marry me. And she has the blessing of the pope himself for this marriage. We are indeed favoured, are we not, my dear?' he finished by caressing Mary Beatrice's cheek with a greasy hand.

She nodded and looked down at the portion of eel pie on her plate. Mary could see that Mary Beatrice was revolted by the dish. Oh, dear! thought Mary. How unhappy she must be.

Trying to say something cheerful, Mary asked, 'What is Italy like?' She immediately saw that it was the wrong thing. Mary Beatrice's eyes welled up with tears and she bit her lip. A cloud of ill humour passed over the duke's face. 'Well, answer her, my dear!' the duke said between bites.

Her eyes glistening with unshed tears, Mary Beatrice whispered, 'Very warm and sunny, with many gardens.'

'We have gardens here,' the duke interrupted. Mary Beatrice drew back from him at the tone.

Mary laid down her knife and spoke up. 'Yes, the gardens at Richmond are lovely. The rose garden is especially beautiful in the summer. You must come and visit us there.'

'No,' the duke interrupted. 'You will visit us here, where your home ought to be.' He cut himself a large piece of cheese from the round wheel and set it on his silver plate.

Mary, who had forgotten to eat, stared at her father. 'Will we be coming here to live with you?' she asked with a mixture of fear and excitement. Anne looked up briefly from her plate full of all the foods on the table.

'No,' he replied sourly, 'but you should. However, the king has said you may make visits to your stepmother and me at regular intervals.'

The rest of the meal passed with the duke doing most of the talking. Afterwards, Mary and Anne kissed their father and stepmother goodnight and went with Mam to their old nursery apartments.

Mam looked very pleased and hummed a little tune as she helped the girls off with their dresses and into their nightgowns. 'What a lovely new stepmother you have,' she observed while pulling a white linen gown over Anne's head.

'Yes,' came Anne's mumbled reply in the folds of the garment. 'But she looked very sad.'

'Oh, don't worry about that. She's homesick, which is only to be expected. I'm sure you will help her feel at home here.'

Then Anne suddenly switched subjects and asked, 'Why were those people burning that straw man? Papa told me not to look. Why?'

Mam's smooth face suddenly wrinkled up fiercely. 'Because they are ignorant fools!'

'Mrs Langford, that will be enough.' Lady Frances stood in the doorway, arms folded across her chest. 'You are dismissed for the night. I will see Lady Mary and Lady Anne into bed.'

Mam swung round and looked ready to do battle, but she stopped herself. Instead she gave a loud 'harrumph' and walked proudly out of the room.

'That woman,' Mary heard each of them mutter about the other as they passed.

Anne, ignoring the conflict, immediately asked her question again, this time of their governess. 'What were those people doing?'

Lady Frances went back to close the bedroom door. 'Come,' she said, 'into bed with you and we'll have a little talk before you sleep.'

The girls climbed up onto the high tester bed and pulled the sheets and blankets over them. Lady Frances pulled the deep blue bed curtains around the bed and then joined them on the bed, arranging her long skirts as best she could.

'I'll explain what I can,' she began, as both girls leaned forward to hear her hushed voice. 'Your father has married a Catholic woman against the king's wishes.'

Mary's eyes widened with fear and she felt a stab of guilt for not praying for her father more often. 'What will the king do?' she asked.

Lady Frances gave a resigned sigh. 'What he always does. Complain about it and then shrug and say we must accept it. Of course, the king himself admires the new duchess's beauty, even if she is only fifteen.'

Poor Mary Beatrice, Mary thought, only four years older than me and so far from home.

'But what does that have to do with the people on the street?' Anne persisted.

'The people of London are angry with the duke and with the king too.' Lady Frances explained. 'Before you were born our country was torn apart by civil war. Many families lost their beloved sons and husbands fighting about whether we should be Protestant or Catholic. The Protestants won. But now, your father appears intent on making us Catholic once more. So the people are protesting, by burning an effigy of the pope.'

Anne wrinkled her pudgy nose. 'What's that?'

'They make a man out of straw, dress him as the pope, and then take him to the bonfire and throw him in to show how much they hate him.'

'They must be very angry,' Mary observed.

'Will they try to hurt Papa or Mary Beatrice, or even us?' Anne asked anxiously.

'No, no,' Lady Frances replied moving closer to embrace Anne. 'There is no need to fear. The palace guards will protect us. You are quite safe.' She reached over and patted Mary's shoulder. 'Now you both need to say your prayers and go to sleep.'

'Please stay with us,' Anne pleaded.

'I will,' Lady Frances replied. 'The trundle bed is made up so I can sleep here too. Now let's ask God to take away your fears and give you a peaceful night's sleep.'

The next day Mary and Anne spent most of their time with Mary Beatrice. Without their father present, Mary Beatrice was much more relaxed. She even smiled a little as they played a card game. One of her ladies-in-waiting, red-headed Sarah Jennings, was lively and chatted away, covering up the silences. By the end of the day, Sarah had them all playing hide and seek in the set of apartments. Eventually they all collapsed in great gales of laughter.

'It is good to see you so merry,' Sarah observed as they all settled themselves around the fire. 'Having your new daughters here will bring you much joy, Your Grace.'

'I only wish they could stay all the time,' Mary Beatrice replied, smiling at Mary and Anne.

'We're not allowed to,' Anne informed her bluntly. 'You're a Catholic and we're Protestant.'

'I know,' Mary Beatrice replied, 'but it hurts your father deeply that he cannot see his daughters.'

There was silence for a few moments as each young person contemplated the situation. Mary genuinely liked her new stepmother, but she knew that living at St James's Palace could quickly become unpleasant. Mary had learned enough about her stepmother from Mam earlier in the day to know that Mary Beatrice was a very devout Catholic. She had even planned to become a nun before the Duke of York asked to marry her. Mary Beatrice had refused his marriage proposal, and only accepted it after the pope told her it was her duty. That worried Mary. It was just as Dr Lake had said; the pope tells

Catholics what to do and they do it because they believe he speaks for God.

* * *

Throughout the following year, Mary and Anne were allowed regular visits to St James's Palace to see their stepmother. While Mary enjoyed these visits, Anne appeared uncomfortable and always complained to Mary afterwards that they shouldn't spend so much time with a Catholic.

'Well, if you don't want to talk to our stepmother, speak to Sarah Jennings instead. She's a Protestant,' Mary responded. 'Besides the duchess never speaks of her religion to me.'

And so they fell into a pattern. The four of them would play cards, do needlework, or go for long walks in the gardens, usually in pairs: Mary and Mary Beatrice speaking excitedly to each other and Sarah Jennings and Anne conversing quietly behind. Mary knew she should be pleased to have her stepmother to herself but she worried about her sister being too friendly with Sarah. Sarah could be sly and Mary suspected that Sarah cared more about being close to the royal family than about Anne herself. But all those concerns fell away at the happy news that Mary Beatrice was expecting a baby.

The Wrong Baptism

(1674 – 1676)

'A baby!' Anne said excitedly. 'May I help care for him?'

Mary laughed along with their stepmother and Sarah Jennings. Anne looked hurt. 'What's wrong with that?' the ten-year-old pouted. 'I love babies.'

Sarah spoke first. 'Nothing at all, Lady Anne. You show good maternal feelings and one day you'll have babies of your own.' Sarah said knowingly. 'But you will also have many servants to help you care for them.'

'Indeed,' Mary Beatrice joined in. 'Babies are a lot of work.'

Anne, still huffy, sat down with a flounce on the yellow and blue upholstered settee. Sarah went over and sat with her, putting her arm around the girl's shoulder.

Mary, annoyed at Sarah's familiarity, almost said something when her stepmother spoke.

'All being well the baby will arrive sometime in January. So I'm going to ask the king for permission for you to come for Christmas and stay until the baby arrives.'

Diverted, Mary hugged the duchess. 'That would be lovely. I do hope you have a boy. I'm sure that will make Papa very happy.'

Sarah Jennings' light laughter caused them both to look her way. 'You have a very generous spirit, Lady Mary,' Sarah said with a sly smile. 'If the duchess does have a boy, he will be in line for the throne ahead of you.'

Mary shrugged with annoyance. 'I don't care about the throne. I don't even want to be a queen. So,' she turned back to her stepmother, 'I'd be very pleased if God gives you a son.'

'May it be so,' Mary Beatrice replied earnestly.

Not only did the king give permission for the girls to come to court for the Christmas season of 1674, but he also ordered that a play be written and Mary and Anne given the lead parts. Mary could hardly believe that she was the one dressed in layers of filmy cloth covered with tiny jewels and standing on a stage before the entire court. As the music began she lost herself in the story of Callisto, the wood nymph, remembering all her lines and dancing gracefully about the stage. The play went well, except when Anne dropped the quiver of arrows she was supposed to hand to Mary. Anne had to chase about the stage to retrieve them. The court laughed good-naturedly but Anne blushed bright red.

'Never mind,' Mary whispered as she took the quiver and continued her dance.

As all the young ladies curtsied at the end of the play, Mary noticed how proud her father looked as he clapped heartily. And the king, still a handsome man in his forties, stood up and called out his hurrahs in a loud voice. Since he stood, so did the rest of the court, including heavily pregnant Mary Beatrice, who struggled to stand up with help from Queen Catherine. Mary's heart swelled with pride. How she wished this moment could go on forever.

At the ball afterwards, Mary danced until dawn, surprised at first that so many young men asked for the privilege of leading her. Even clumsy Anne was led out often to the dance floor, until she complained she was too tired. Mary then began to realise that it was because she and her sister were the duke's daughters, but she didn't care. The play and the ball had made this the most wonderful Christmas she had ever had.

* * *

The rest of the time passed quietly in Mary Beatrice's apartment waiting for the arrival of the baby. When the labour pains began, Mary and Anne were ushered to their own apartment while the duchess's ladies helped her into bed. Both girls felt a little put out because they knew that the birth would be a public affair, with many of the king's court gathering to witness the royal baby's arrival. Now thirteen, Mary felt she was old enough to be part of the event. Instead, she joined Anne at the frosted window, kneeling on the padded window seat where they watched the coaches bounce along the frozen rutted drive up to the palace.

Not many hours later a servant arrived to conduct Mary and Anne back to their stepmother's bedchamber. The crowds of well-dressed ladies and gentlemen moved aside to let the girls pass through. Anne was squeezing Mary's hand in excitement.

'I want so much to hold him,' she whispered to Mary.

Just then they passed an older man, who said to his wife, 'Well, no need to stay any longer. It's just a girl. No one will be celebrating tonight.'

Oh, dear! thought Mary. Poor Papa and poor Mary Beatrice.

As they arrived at the doorway they had to stand aside as the king led out some of the Privy Councillors from the bedchamber. 'Well, she's young,' King Charles was saying to them. 'There'll be many more babies, I'm sure. Come along and we'll drink a toast to her anyway. Ah, the young ladies,' he stopped when he spied Mary and Anne. 'Do go in and comfort your stepmother. She's a little upset and needs her daughters. Go along, now.' And he moved aside for them. Both girls gave the king a quick curtsy and then ran in to see their new sister.

Mary Beatrice was sitting up in the tester bed leaning tiredly against the pillows, tears glistening on her cheeks. Beside her, the duke was patting her hand and murmuring softly to her. Both looked over as the girls came to stand at the end of the enormous curtained bed.

'There you are,' their father said. 'Come round this way,' he said letting go of his wife's hand and motioning them to his side of the bed.

'Where's the baby?' Anne asked eagerly.

'Here,' said Sarah appearing beside them with a tiny bundle in her arms.

'Give Lady Anne the child,' the duke directed and, as Sarah placed the baby in Anne's arms, he ordered everyone to leave the room, asking Sarah to draw the bed curtains before she left.

Sarah wore a secret smile as she carried out the duke's orders and Mary wondered what was going on. As the heavy bedroom door closed with a deliberate bang, a secret door in the panelled wall behind the headboard opened, revealing a Catholic priest dressed in a black cassock and felt hat.

With a nod from the duke, the priest came around to the other side of the bed and reached outside the bed curtains to carefully draw a small table with a washbasin full of water close to the bed. Then he held out his arms for the baby. Transfixed by the priest, Anne didn't resist when the duke took the baby from her and handed her across to the priest.

Horrified, Mary watched as the priest proceeded to baptise the baby with the words of the Catholic rite, naming the child Catherine Laura. She turned to speak to her father but the words never came out. The duke glared at her and her stepmother sent her a pleading look. When the priest finished, he handed the crying baby to Mary Beatrice. Bowing to the duke and duchess, he left the same way he had arrived.

'Now, I'll not hear a word said about this,' the duke said sternly to his daughters. 'Both your stepmother and I wanted our daughter to be baptised in our religion. No one else needs to know. Is that clear?'

Both Mary and Anne nodded mutely, afraid to speak. After dutifully kissing Mary Beatrice and their new sister, they returned to their apartments.

'That was very wrong,' Anne whispered as they walked down the long corridor still full of people talking and laughing. 'Papa had no right to do that and Mary Beatrice should not have asked him. They are both wicked.'

'Hush,' Mary whispered urgently. 'People will hear you. I know it was wrong, but Papa told us not to tell. We can't disobey him, can we?'

* * *

Still very uneasy about what had happened, the girls returned to Richmond Palace the next day with their governess and Mam. Subdued, Mary trailed after the other girls as they saw one tutor after another for their lessons. Anne stayed in bed, announcing she was unwell and Mam let her stay there. Mary suspected Anne just didn't want to study because it was too difficult for her weak eyes.

A week later Lady Frances arrived at the girls' apartment and shooed all the servants out. Mary could tell by the look on their governess's face that the secret had got out. She hung her head as Lady Frances questioned them and gave mumbled replies. Anne was much more willing to tell all.

'Never mind,' said Lady Frances at the end of the tale. 'You had little choice, but now we must return to London. The king has demanded that the child be baptised in the Anglican Church and you are to be her godparents.'

'What does a godparent do?' Anne wanted to know.

'They teach about the true faith,' Mary explained. 'We will be able to tell Catherine, when she is older, that she must believe in Jesus Christ alone and not think that taking the sacraments or doing good works will save her from her sins.'

Lady Frances nodded. 'Now, let's get ready to return to London.'

* * *

The baptism was conducted by Bishop Compton, the newly appointed Bishop of London, in the Royal Chapel at St James's Palace. Neither the duke nor the duchess attended, but the girls' handsome cousin, the Duke of Monmouth, became baby Catherine's third godparent. He winked playfully at Mary and Anne, as he made his vows.

Sadly, Catherine only lived nine months, dying of unexplained convulsions in September of 1675. Everyone mourned the loss of the little girl, especially her mother, who was now expecting her second child.

During this time Mary and Anne carried on with their lives at Richmond Palace, with occasional visits to St James's Palace to see Mary Beatrice. They saw little of their father because of his duties in the navy, or at least that is what the duchess said. But she was sad much of the time and Mary wondered if the gossip she had heard about her father meeting other women was true. Worried about upsetting Mary Beatrice even more, Mary kept those thoughts to herself.

* * *

The following spring Bishop Compton paid a visit to Richmond Palace. He arrived too late to lead the evening prayer service, but the next morning Dr Lake took a seat on the benches and the bishop led the household in morning prayers. He was dressed in a white surplice over his black gown with his shoulder-length grey hair hanging neatly below his black cap. After the simple service of praise, prayer and scripture reading, they were dismissed to go to the dining room and break their fast.

Mary was chatting with Anne Villiers and Frances Apsley as they made their way arm in arm out of the chapel when Dr Lake called her aside.

'Lady Mary, Bishop Compton would like to speak with you.'

All three girls looked surprised, but then Frances released Mary and took Anne's arm and said they would see Mary later. Mary turned to the bishop who bowed to her and suggested they sit in the chairs at the back of the chapel. Mary did so uneasily, thinking back to the conversation she had with Dr Lake on those chairs a few years ago.

Professing Faith

(1676-1677)

'Lady Mary,' Bishop Compton began. 'King Charles has asked me to take over as your spiritual advisor.'

Mary took a quick glance at Dr Lake to see how he was receiving the news. Was he in trouble with the king? But the older man was nodding and smiling.

'Now that you are turning fourteen, the king feels it's time that you joined the church. So I'm here to see how you are progressing in your understanding of the faith.'

Mary almost groaned aloud. This was an examination that no one had told her to prepare for. Her feelings must have shown on her face, because the bishop smiled encouragingly.

'There is no need for concern. All you need to do is answer your catechism questions for me. Dr Lake tells me you know them well.'

Mary was relieved. 'I think so, Your Grace.'

'Let me hear you say the Ten Commandments,' the bishop said.

Mary recited the commandments without error.

'Well done,' Bishop Compton commended her. 'Now let me hear your catechism. What do you chiefly learn by these commandments?'

Mary knew the prescribed answer. 'I learn two things: my duty towards God, and my duty towards my neighbour.'

'What is your duty towards God?'

'My duty towards God, is to believe in him, to fear him, and to love him with all my heart, with all my mind, with all my soul, and with all my strength; to worship him, to give him thanks, to put my whole trust in him, to call upon him, to honour his holy name and his Word, and to serve him truly all the days of my life.'

'What is your duty towards your neighbour?'

'My duty towards my neighbour is to love him as myself, and to do to all men as I would they should do unto me.'[2]

And so they continued. All the way through, Mary was able to answer with confidence. Bishop Compton nodded with satisfaction.

'You have learned your lessons well and what's more you appear to have a mature understanding of the doctrines of the church. Tell me, Lady Mary, do you feel ready to join the church, to take your place at the communion rail?'

'Oh, yes,' Mary began enthusiastically, but then she stopped herself. 'But I still sin a great deal,' she confessed. 'Shouldn't I wait until I'm a better Christian?'

Bishop Compton leaned forward and took one of her hands in his. 'My dear child, none of us will ever

---

[2] Book of Common Prayer, 1662, A Catechism

be without sin until we reach heaven. But remember that Christ has paid the penalty for our sin. What is important is that you choose to serve God, repenting of your sin and striving to live a life that pleases him. Have you done that?'

'Yes, I have,' Mary replied quietly.

'Then I will speak with your father and ask his permission for your confirmation.'

'Oh, no! My father will never consent to me being confirmed in the Church of England.' Mary was distressed to think of the unkind words her father might say to the bishop.

'Do not worry, Lady Mary. I will approach your father first, because he is your father and deserves to know what is planned for his daughter. The king is still your guardian and has already decided it should be so if you are ready. After all, you have been raised in the Protestant faith and must remain so, for the sake of the succession, as well as for the sake of your soul.'

Bishop Compton left that morning to return to London. Mary heard no more on the subject until the following week when a servant arrived during a French lesson to ask her to come to the library. Surprised, she followed the servant down the corridor, her silk slippers barely making a whisper on the wooden floor. As the servant opened the door to the library she saw her father standing by the marble fireplace, flanked on either side by large glass doors. One of the doors stood open to the April breeze and the scent of the colourful spring flowers in the terrace planters wafted into the room. Colonel and Lady Villiers were standing uncomfortably to one side by the colonel's large oak desk, appearing to study the large oriental rug covering the wooden floor. All three looked around to the door.

'Daughter, come in, come in,' the duke said, advancing across the room.

Mary sank into a deep curtsy and then rose to give the duke a kiss on his cheek. Mary was surprised to realise she was now almost as tall as her father. Suddenly she felt grown-up. As he led her over to the deep red settee, the duke began to explain his visit.

'I brought you a birthday present,' he said handing her a small velvet bag with drawstrings. 'Sit down and open it.'

Mary did as she was told, and a pearl necklace tumbled out onto her lap. 'It's beautiful, Papa. Thank you.'

She threw her arms about his neck and hugged him. He laughed and returned her hug. Then Mary noticed her governess, still standing, watching them with disapproval.

What's going on, Mary wondered as she drew back from the duke. Papa has never made a fuss over my birthday before.

'Did you come all this way just to give me a birthday present?' she asked lightly.

'Of course. I have the loveliest of daughters and she deserves to have gifts,' her father responded in the same tone. But then he sobered. 'There is another matter we should discuss.'

Mary felt her stomach begin to knot up with anxiety, and she fingered the necklace as she waited for the duke to continue.

'Bishop Compton has been to see me, telling some sort of nonsense about you joining the Church of England. Surely that can't be true of a daughter of mine, I thought. So I decided to come to find out for myself.'

Mary swallowed. She hated to make her father lose his temper, so she tried in her most reasonable voice to say, 'Yes, Papa. I must join the church,' and she finished quickly as she saw the colour rising in her father's face. 'Because I love God and want to serve him.'

'So, your father and stepmother don't love God and don't serve him?' he sneered. 'You have been sadly misinformed. The Catholic religion is the only true one, not this new faith.' He rose from the settee and towered over her. 'You would rather join a heretical church than see your soul safe in the true church! Let's see what the king has to say about this.' Then he turned and strode out of the room.

Mary burst into tears and Lady Frances rushed over to the settee to gather her in her arms. Mary buried her face in her governess's shoulder and sobbed until she could cry no more. Fumbling for a handkerchief, she began to wipe her eyes and blow her nose and all this while Lady Frances made small comforting noises.

'Can he really stop my confirmation?' Mary asked.

'Of course not,' Lady Frances replied firmly. 'The king has already decided and your father, despite all his faults, does listen to his brother, the king. Just be patient and it will all happen as it should.' Lady Frances said as she smoothed out Mary's abundant chestnut-coloured hair. 'Meanwhile, you must continue to study the Scriptures and understand clearly what you are about to do.'

'But what about the fifth commandment?' Mary asked, stifling a sob. 'Am I not breaking it, disobeying my father's wishes?'

Lady Frances sighed deeply, looking over to her husband for help.

The colonel, who rarely spoke to any of the young ladies that lived in his home, cleared his throat. 'Lady Mary, as I see it your first responsibility is to God. He is to be obeyed when men get things wrong, even a father. Sadly, I believe your father will have to answer before God for his attempt to dissuade you from the right course of action.'

Having said such a long speech, the colonel bowed to them both and left the room.

Lady Frances nodded. 'Serving God and your king are your first priorities, especially when your father is in error.'

Mary knew they were right. But why did it have to hurt so much to do what was right?

Word came the following week. The king commanded that Mary should come to London to be confirmed and then remain as part of the court in London. The packing began immediately with Mam in her element ordering the servants about.

'Where will I live?' Mary wanted to know with some anxiety as she sat with her governess and sister in the reception room. The girls were supposed to be working on their needlework, but not much was getting done.

'Your stepmother has requested that you stay with her. She would like your companionship.' Lady Frances replied as she scanned the letter from the king's secretary once more. She had brought it to show Mary.

'Will I move there too?' Anne asked, glad to let her wrinkled linen sampler sit on her lap. Her poor eyesight made her needlework a messy and unrewarding chore.

'No, you're still too young, Lady Anne, but you do have permission to visit your sister and stepmother from time to time. You too will need to be confirmed in the church in a couple of years.'

Anne nodded vigorously. 'I would do it now, if Dr Lake would let me. I know my catechism and I want to show Papa that I won't be persuaded to become a Catholic either.'

Lady Frances shook her head. 'Lady Anne, while I agree with your desire to serve God, you must be careful to still have respect for your father. He is to be honoured wherever possible.'

Mary and Anne exchanged confused looks. It all seemed to be so complicated, more complicated than either girl could say. So they said nothing.

* * *

Mary was torn as she left Richmond Palace in May. Watching the large red brick palace recede as the royal barge sailed up the River Thames, she had an urge to jump out and swim back. Maybe if she hid in her bedchamber the way her sister Anne often did, she wouldn't have to leave her home. On the other hand, she was looking forward to her confirmation, when she could profess her faith and take her place at the communion rail. And she did want to see her stepmother. Mary Beatrice had lost two infants now and she grieved deeply. She seemed more like a sister than a mother and Mary was eager to see her.

Mary arrived in London with her new group of ladies-in-waiting and her governess. Lady Frances only planned to remain for the confirmation service the following morning and then return to Richmond. To Mary's joy, Anne Villiers had been selected to be one of her companions, but Mary was very sad that Frances Apsley had been called home to care for her ailing father. And worst of all Anne's older sister, Betty Villiers, was also sent to serve at court as a companion. Mary had complained privately to Anne Villiers about having no say about who was appointed to her household, and while Anne was a sympathetic listener, there was little either young woman could do to change the fact.

The confirmation service was a private one in the Chapel Royal, with just her ladies, her governess and Bishop Compton present. She knelt on a cushion on the stone floor in front of the bishop as he laid his hands on her head and prayed for her, his deep voice echoing in the almost empty chapel.

'Almighty and ever living God, who hast vouchsafed to regenerate this thy servant by water and the Holy Ghost, and hast given unto her forgiveness of all her sins: Strengthen her, we beseech thee, O Lord, with the Holy Ghost the Comforter, and daily increase in her thy manifold gifts of grace; the spirit of wisdom and understanding; the spirit of counsel and ghostly strength; the spirit of knowledge and true godliness; and fill her, O Lord, with the spirit of thy holy fear, now and for ever.'[3]

Mary answered, 'Amen.'

Then she took communion for the first time, accepting the small wafer and the ornate silver goblet for a sip of red wine with appropriate solemnity. As Bishop Compton spoke the words of the service, Mary contemplated the fact of Jesus' terrible death

---

[3] From 'The Order of Confirmation' in the *Book of Common Prayer of the Churches of England and Ireland*.

on the cross, humbly thanking God for his mercy and forgiveness. Afterwards, if anyone asked her what it was like she could only use the words from the catechism - 'it strengthened and refreshed my soul.'

* * *

Mary spent the next year in Mary Beatrice's company at the court, carefully avoiding the discussion of church and religion. She saw almost nothing of her father or the king. They were taken up with the on again, off again wars with France and the Dutch, when they weren't enjoying the entertainments of the court. Mary was uncomfortable with how most people conducted themselves at court, gambling away their money and behaving sinfully with each other's husbands or wives. Both Catholic and Protestants misbehaved with the same careless regard for the sermons they heard on Sundays. So Mary did her best to live quietly; spending her time sewing, playing cards with her stepmother, taking long walks, writing copious letters to her sister and Frances Apsley, and spending some private time in prayer and Bible reading.

As time went on Mary almost had the impression that everyone was waiting for something, but she didn't know what. Her stepmother looked at her with some speculation at times, but refused to say why. Even Sarah, Mary Beatrice's lady-in-waiting, dropped odd hints now and then with a secret smile. Mary was unnerved, but afraid to ask what it was all about.

The Terrible Announcement

(October 1677)

The brown autumn leaves crunched under Mary's timber-heeled shoes as she walked beside her stepmother. Here and there the cool breezes whipped up a swirl of the dying oak leaves, that danced across the pathway and off onto the green lawns of St James's Park. The group of women pulled their light cloaks closer around them.

'Do you need to rest, or turn back to the palace?' Mary asked Mary Beatrice anxiously. Her stepmother was once more expecting a baby.

Mary Beatrice leaned on Mary's arm while Sarah and the other ladies-in-waiting hovered close by. 'No, no,' she sighed quietly. 'It's finally dry after so much rain. I'd like to enjoy the sun a little longer.'

Mary glanced over at Sarah's disapproving look and for once agreed with her. The duchess looked pale and tired. However, they walked on a little further between the two rows of oak trees that King Charles had planted when he was crowned sixteen years ago. But their walk was interrupted by the arrival of a messenger telling them that the king and his court were returning from Newcastle to London today and all were invited to a banquet tomorrow evening.

'I wonder what brought His Majesty back early from the horse racing?' Mary wondered aloud as they headed back to the palace.

'Never mind that,' Sarah replied excitedly. 'We should all be thinking about what we're going to wear, not to mention who we will sit with.'

Mary exchanged amused glances with her stepmother. They both knew that Sarah had a certain John Churchill in mind, who served the Duke of York as Gentleman of the Bedchamber. When the duke was in residence in St James's Palace, Captain Churchill had been using his spare time to court Sarah.

* * *

The next evening, Mary arrived at the Banquet Hall dressed in a new bodice and skirt of red and white silk that the king had sent for her to wear. The ladies had all admired its fine lace trim around the deep curved neckline and three-quarter sleeves. Mary Beatrice suggested she wear the pearl necklace her father had given her and Mam dressed her chestnut hair with small ribbons and a jewelled comb. She tried to take a deep breath as she stood in the door way, but her tight bodice only allowed a few short ones. Abandoned by her ladies-in-waiting, who had gone ahead into the Banquet Hall to claim good seats, Mary followed a servant, dressed in the royal livery, to the antechamber where the rest of the royal family had gathered.

Mary gave a general curtsy to all as she entered the room. Her stepmother and the queen, sitting off to one side on elaborate upholstered chairs acknowledged her with smiles. Queen Catherine, who appeared tiny next to the duchess, was often ill at ease with the English language and customs, but was always kind to Mary. Mary knew well how much the queen longed for children. Each time she had given birth, her babies had only lived a month or two. So the queen spent her time fussing over her sister-in-law with each of her pregnancies. Lady Anne sat by the fire looking bored.

Milling about in the centre of the room were the king's dogs. Some were small lap dogs and others large hunting dogs. A few came over to sniff her skirt, but Mary spoke sternly to the youngest one of the pack who was about to jump up for some personal attention. Discouraged, the young pup returned to his mother who lay by the fireplace.

The king and Mary's father stood on the other side of the room deep in conversation with a third man, who was both shorter and much more plainly dressed than either of the royal brothers. His dark blue long waistcoat and knee breeches were without the fashionable lace or bows that most men wore. His long-sleeved white shirt sleeves billowed out from the shoulders and his simple white cravat hung in two wide strips of cloth. His long chestnut brown hair hung in curls past his shoulders.

'Ah, my dear niece,' the king said, turning as Mary entered the room. 'I knew that dress would suit you.'

'Thank you, Your Majesty,' Mary murmured as she curtsied deeply once more. 'It was very kind...' but she got no further, for the king continued.

'Come, meet your cousin, William. He's come all the way from the Netherlands to visit us.' The king motioned for a younger man to step forward.

Mary was puzzled. She knew she had a cousin in the Low Countries, but she had thought that England was still at war with the Dutch people. So why was the king entertaining their leader?

'Well, my dear, talk to him. He won't bite you.'

Mary gave her cousin a quick curtsy. William bowed politely in return. Up close, Mary was struck with how much he resembled her father and the king. But before they could exchange any words, the steward came in to lead the royal family into the Banquet Hall.

The horns in the gallery played the royal fanfare as King Charles swept in with his usual grace with Queen Catherine on his arm. Chairs and benches scraped the wooden floor in a sound almost as loud as the horns when everyone stood for the king. Then the Duke of York offered his wife his arm, which she took gratefully and moved with slow grace to the door. William offered his arm without a word and Mary set her hand on it. As she did so, she realised just how short her cousin was. She could look right over his head. Oh, dear! she thought. This is going to be a very dull evening.

Tall candelabras stood in the corners of the Banquet Hall burning brightly along with the ones hanging from the painted ceiling. The smoke from the candle created a haze and made it difficult for Mary to see very far ahead. So she concentrated on making sure her gown didn't snag on any of the furniture.

Once they were all seated at the high table at the end of the hall, the king called for the feast to begin. The servants began to bring in the platters of food.

The king turned his attention to his yapping dogs that had followed and were demanding their share of the food on the table. 'Here you go, you noisy mongrels,' he said affectionately tossing some chunks of meat to them.

William let out a noise of disgust, and Mary stole a panicked look to see if the king had heard. The king, however, was laughing at the dogs' antics and pointing them out to the queen. Mary turned once more as William began to cough.

'Are you well?' she asked as the cough persisted.

William nodded, reaching for his silver goblet to take a drink. Recovering his breath, he murmured, 'The smoke from the candles bothers me.'

Mary didn't know what to reply to that so she busied herself by selecting some pigeon pie from a serving platter nearby. She nodded to the servant who offered to pour her some wine. She noticed that William hardly took any food and seemed rather tense. Glancing once more at the king who was telling jokes and laughing loudly, she wondered why she was left to talk to this reserved cousin.

After waiting for him to introduce a new subject of conversation, Mary decided to ask him about his homeland. But before she could get the words out, William suddenly asked her a question.

'Do you attend church regularly?'

When she nodded, he wanted to know why. 'To worship God,' Mary replied.

'Not just because you must, as the king's niece?' William appeared very earnest.

'No, I worship God because I love him and want to serve him.'

'Tell me what you learn from your chaplain,' William encouraged. He then turned his attention to his plate while Mary recited some of the catechism. She was unsure if he was listening until she hesitated and he supplied the missing word.

Her recitation came to an end when William started to cough again. As he struggled for breath, the steward came forward and offered him more wine. He tried to drink, but he only coughed all the more. Then a red-headed man about William's age appeared at the table and offered to lead the prince outside for some fresh air. Mary watched them go with relief.

King Charles turned to her and shook his head with smile. 'Never mind, my dear,' he said, 'he will return.'

Mary almost sighed aloud, but caught herself as the king watched her carefully. 'Learn to like him, my dear. He's not so bad.'

Mary puzzled over that remark for the rest of the evening, but forgot about it the next day as she listened to her ladies chatter. They were gathered around her chamber sewing bed curtains and trading thoughts on the banquet and various people's behaviours.

'Did you see the Duke of Monmouth and how he carried on with the queen's new lady-in-waiting? And with his wife sitting there too!' one said with a giggle.

'He can get away with much, being the king's son, even if he is only the son of one of the king's mistresses,' another replied. 'And what about Sarah and her captain! I'll lay odds they will sneak away to get married before long.'

'They wouldn't dare without my father's permission,' Mary protested.

'Sarah would dare just about anything,' came the laughing response.

Just then the door to the chamber opened and in walked the Duke of York. All the young women rose hastily from their seats and curtsied deeply.

The duke acknowledged them with a nod and then said, 'Daughter, I wish to speak to you alone.'

Startled, Mary led the way to her bedchamber, still clutching her length of green brocade fabric and her needle. Her father followed her into the inner room and shut the door. Mary turned to study his face, trying to determine if he was angry with her.

'I have news for you. The happiest news a young woman wants to hear,' he said with some irony.

Mary stared into her father's grim face as her breathing quickened and her stomach began to tighten.

'You are to be married in two weeks' time to your cousin, William. The king has given his permission.'

Mary was too stunned to speak, so her father continued, this time pacing up and down the room. 'I don't approve, but the king has told me I must obey, and so do you. I'd much prefer you marry the Dauphin of France because he's Catholic rather than that stern Calvinist cousin of yours. But we need to end this war with the Netherlands. It's too costly and this is apparently the price William has asked for peace.'

Mary burst into tears and sat down abruptly on her bed. 'I'm only fifteen,' she wailed. 'How can the king be so cruel?'

Her father stopped his pacing and came over to her. He patted her head gently and said, 'God appoints the king. When he speaks we must obey. Besides, your stepmother was your age when I married her. You'll be fine. Now dry your tears and I'll send the duchess to you to discuss your wedding clothes.'

As her father rose to leave, she asked desperately, 'Couldn't the wedding be delayed until next year?'

'No. William insists on the 4th of November so you can both leave for The Hague immediately afterwards.'

'No! I can't leave England and my family so soon!' Mary collapsed on the bed, sobbing into the embroidered pillows.

* * *

With unbelievable swiftness, the two weeks disappeared in a flurry of formal and informal receptions, fevered measuring and sewing of wedding clothes, and lots of laughter and chatter among Mary's ladies-in-waiting. Through it all, Mary couldn't stop her tears. When she woke in the morning, her first thought was to count the days until she had to leave her home. As the morning wore on, she thought about the strange place she would be living in very soon. When she stood by her soon-to-be husband, a head shorter than her, she thought about this stranger she would have to live with for the rest of her life. How could she love someone whom she knew nothing about? And yet everyone around her thought this was the most wonderful thing that could happen.

Every new thought brought fresh tears. Mary had hoped to find some peace and deliverance as she prayed at the morning and evening prayer services. But God seemed not to hear her pleas for rescue, so she left the chapel in as much distress as when she entered.

When the 4th of November arrived, Mary knew her eyes were red and swollen, turning her pretty face into one of misery. Even the new yellow brocade dress did nothing to sooth the fear and panic in the pit of her stomach. As she stood with William in front of Bishop Compton, she could barely breathe, never mind get the words out for the ceremony. Behind her stood the king and queen and her father and stepmother. Her sister, Anne, had taken ill and couldn't attend. The king was the only cheerful one present and he kept up a running commentary as the ceremony progressed. Then, suddenly, it was over and Mary was a married woman. I can't do this. God help me! Mary kept thinking and praying, just before she felt herself grow faint.

* * *

Later that night, Mary was prepared for bed by the queen and the duchess. They had sent all the ladies-in-waiting away to give Mary some peace. As she stood on the woven carpet of running deer and other forest animals, the queen undid the buttons at the back of her bodice and the duchess gently pulled it forward. Tears splashed down on her stepmother's hands.

'Oh, my dear child! Please don't take on so,' the duchess said as she gave Mary a hug.

Queen Catherine, who had been untying the skirt, stopped and came around front. 'You will make yourself ill,' she advised in heavily accented English. 'And it will do no good. Both your stepmother and I had to leave our homes and families to marry. It is the lot of princesses to do so. You must accept your duty.'

'No, I won't,' Mary replied childishly. 'It's too hard, too awful. You both were able to come to England. I have to leave it,' she finished with a wail.

'Stop this at once,' Mary Beatrice said, taking Mary by the shoulders. 'You are now a married woman. God has ordained this for you and you must accept it.' Then, changing her grip to yet another hug, she whispered into Mary's ear, 'I will write to you daily and so will your sister, so you will always have news of us and home. Now let's finish getting you ready for bed. Your husband will be arriving very soon.'

Looking for Love

(November 1677)

Mary stood on the deck of the *Katherine* watching the coastline of England grow smaller on the horizon. The fierce wind swirled around her, flinging a fine mist of salt water in her face, while the dark storm clouds gathered overhead. Clutching the railing, she realised once more she had no say in her own life. She was practically a captive, being carried away to a foreign land. Oddly her tears had stopped as she had boarded the ship. She had just learned that her governess had died of smallpox and her sister, Lady Anne, was very ill with the same disease. Now that her grief for Lady Frances and her sister was added to her own sorry plight, Mary found herself numb and unable to cry anymore.

'Your Highness,' Anne Villiers shouted above the wind. 'The prince told me to make sure you stayed in your cabin. He fears for your safety.'

'I'm not going to fall overboard,' Mary retorted. 'Besides he's not even on the ship,' she continued as they both looked over at the sister ship *Mary* sailing not far ahead. Given the poor weather conditions, William thought they should sail separately in case of disaster. Mary briefly hoped that if one ship must perish that it would be hers. Other than the inconvenience of undoing the alliance between the English and the Dutch, Mary doubted William would miss her.

'Please, Your Highness, I promised the prince,' Anne pleaded. Mary looked at her lady-in-waiting's pale face, and Mary's despair melted into concern for her grieving friend.

'Very well,' Mary agreed and followed Anne to their cabin across the sloping deck. While Mary's sea legs were steady, Anne's were not and she clutched at ropes and poles as she lurched with the movement of the ship. Coming up behind her, Mary steadied Anne until they reached their cabin.

Once inside, they both tumbled onto the bed when the ship gave a violent lurch. Anne bumped her head on the cabin wall and Mary landed on top of her. After a few seconds they both began to laugh, which turned hysterical as Mary rolled off and lay laughing beside Anne. Anne in turn began to recall the chaos when all the ladies boarded the ship and some of the more ridiculous demands they made about their cabins, which only fed their laughter until they were both gasping for air and holding their sore sides. When they finally subsided the young women lay staring up at the cabin ceiling, watching the lantern swaying, casting odd shadows as it moved.

'I feel badly for laughing like that,' Mary apologised. 'I didn't mean to make light of your grief.'

Anne didn't look at her, but said quietly, 'My mother was always quoting the proverb that laughter is the best medicine. I know you miss her as much as I do.'

Mary said nothing, but reached out and squeezed Anne's hand.

A loud knock sounded at the door, at that moment, that made both of them jump. Struggling to sit up, Mary called out, 'Enter.'

Anne managed to right herself too, just as the wooden door swung inward and a rush of wind and water came in with the captain of the ship.

'Sorry to disturb you, Your Highness,' the broadly built Dutchman began with a deferential nod of his head. 'You and your ladies must keep to your cabins. The winds are strengthening and I can only hope we make land before it blows into a gale. I must apologise, but my cook cannot prepare food in this weather since his help is needed elsewhere. Please, for your own safety, stay in here. I will let you know when we are close to land.'

He left as soon as he finished his speech.

Anne clutched at Mary in terror. 'Will we be lost at sea?'

Trying to calm her own fears, Mary patted Anne's hand and said, 'We should pray for safety.' Together they knelt at the bedside, clutching at the bedclothes as the ship rocked and groaned, and prayed that both ships would reach a safe harbour.

* * *

Several hours later, the captain returned with the news that the Maas River was blocked with ice, so they had sailed down the coast to a small village. Everyone would be taken ashore by small boats.

Mary didn't quite take it all in, until she found herself on a wooden seat being lowered over the side of the ship to a waiting boat below. Terrified, she clung to the sturdy ropes as the wind whipped her cloak about her. When all her ladies had been lowered down too, the sailors pulled on the oars with all their strength against the bitter wind. Within a short time, they ran aground several metres from the shore and the women were forced to leave the boats and wade through the water. The shock of the icy water urged Mary forward as she pulled on her dragging skirt and cloak. By the time she reached the shore she had lost feeling in her feet and she tumbled down onto the sandy beach. She nearly landed face down, but a pair of strong hands caught her around the waist and hoisted her up. Suddenly she found herself carried in a man's arms, his head bent against the wind. She tried to help by pulling her dragging cloak around her.

'Leave off or you'll have us both down,' William's voice urged her. 'Just be calm and I'll get you to safety.'

* * *

Mary woke in a warm feather bed with no memory of the rescue. As she stretched she admired the green silk damask bed curtains and canopy trimmed with gold cord. Sitting up, she peered around the room, taking in the dainty black lacquer furniture and the scenes painted right on the walls and ceiling. Then she noticed Anne Villiers stirring in one of the overstuffed chairs by the white marble fireplace.

'Oh!' Anne sat up suddenly. 'Your Highness, you're awake. I'm sorry, I must have dozed off.' Anne leapt up and opened the heavy draperies letting the weak sunshine through the frost-covered glass. 'I'll tell the servants to prepare a bath for you and some dinner. You must be very hungry.'

Mary laughed at Anne's running commentary. 'Please, slow down a moment. How did I get here?' She patted the bed, inviting Anne to sit down.

Anne complied and began a brief explanation. 'I don't remember much myself,' she admitted, arranging her long skirts around her. 'I know coaches were waiting for us, but it was a long walk through the sand. I fell asleep during the journey and only remember a nice red-headed man helping me up the palace stairs.'

Then Anne smiled. 'I do remember the prince carried you all the way, first to the coaches and then up the stairs and into your bedchamber. He wouldn't allow anyone else to touch you.'

Mary leaned back against the pillows in surprise. 'William? But he's short and sickly. Didn't he cough a lot in that wind and cold?'

Anne's eyes were bright with amusement. 'The prince is a soldier and surprisingly strong. But he was very gentle with you. I think he might really care about you.'

Mary made a dismissive noise. 'I'm just a pawn to him, part of the game plan to end a war. He can't afford to have anything happen to me without ruining the alliance.'

Anne didn't argue. Instead, she helped Mary into her robe and led her through a dressing room to the bathroom. There, Mary was amazed to see a large marble tub standing next to the wall with pipes running along it. The pipes ended with golden taps that poured steaming water into the tub.

'Isn't this wonderful? No more heavy buckets for the servants to carry. Just turn on the tap,' Anne enthused.

Mary touched the water. 'Oh, it's lovely and warm! I must try it.' She quickly disrobed and stepped in the deliciously warm water. She relaxed in the deep tub while Anne continued the tale of their remarkable journey north from their landing to Honselersdijk Palace near The Hague. Just as Mary was emerging from the tub into a warm robe one of the Dutch servants had brought, Mam rushed into the room.

'There you are! No one told me you had woken up! It's been almost two days and I was worried. These Dutch people have no notion of how to care for you and didn't even send for a doctor after such a terrible journey. I was so worried about my little princess,' she said before finally taking a breath.

Mary reached over and hugged Mam. 'There, there. See I'm just fine, especially after such a lovely bath. Now I'd like something to eat.' She kept an arm around Mam and led her out to the dressing room. Anne followed with a look of amusement.

After dressing and eating, Mary was ready to explore her new home. Her ladies were all gathered in her audience chamber, sitting about on the blue and yellow upholstered furniture, some reading letters from home that had followed them on a courier ship. Blue silk damask fabric covered the walls and made up the draperies that framed the large windows overlooking the garden. Some portraits hung on the walls, but Mary had no time to examine them. Her ladies crowded around her, full of complaints and stories.

'Our rooms are too small.'

'The servants hardly speak English and they don't do what I tell them.'

'I'm still so ill from that terrible crossing.'

'These Dutch people scrub everything. They insist I take off my shoes.'

'My aunt has written and told me all three of her children died of the smallpox. I want to go home.'

Fifteen-year-old Mary stood in their midst overwhelmed by the sudden realisation that everyone expected her to fix all these problems. There was no governess or stepmother to go to for advice or help. A feeling of panic began to rise inside her. She was too young for all this and to be married too. Suddenly all the lovely effects of the long sleep and warm bath melted away and she could feel a wave of tears building up behind her eyes.

She rushed into her study, a small room off her audience chamber, and burst into tears. Why had God allowed her to be sent here: married to a man she didn't like, in charge of complaining women and all in a place where she didn't even speak the language. She cried long and hard, wallowing in her misery.

She didn't hear Anne come in until she stood beside her. Tears running down her face, Mary looked at the letter Anne held out to her.

'These might help, Your Highness. Letters from your father and stepmother and one from your sister, Anne, too. She is well again, by all reports.'

Mary managed a watery smile as she took the thick folded pages. 'Thank you.'

Anne continued to stand, looking uncertain. 'Your Highness, Dr Hooper is here. He has asked to speak with you.' As Mary shook her head, Anne suggested, 'Maybe he could help you?'

Mary sighed deeply. 'Very well, show him in. He might as well see me at my worst.'

Anne returned with the short, round clergyman a moment later. Mary had wiped her face and sat up as regally as possible in the upholstered yellow and mauve print chair. Anne left again as Dr Hooper bowed low, causing his periwig to shift dangerously. Mary invited him to sit down.

After straightening his long black gown, Dr Hooper looked at Mary sympathetically. 'Your Highness has been having a difficult time.'

She nodded, not trusting herself to speak.

'Your Highness,' he began and then hesitated. Moistening his lips, he began again. 'Forgive my bluntness, but I must address you on the subject of your marriage.'

'Isn't it rather too late?' Mary asked with some bitterness.

'No, now is just the right time. Your marriage was arranged so quickly that little heed was given to instructing you in your duties as a wife. And I would be failing you as your chaplain to ignore that omission. Your Highness knows there were necessary and good reasons for your marriage, both political and religious. But have you considered your personal role? What Scripture requires of you as a wife?'

Mary shifted uncomfortably. 'I'm not sure what you mean.'

'Even though you didn't choose your husband, you are still required to respect him. St Paul is very clear in Ephesians when he says 'Wives, submit to your own husbands, as to the Lord.' You must show the prince your love and devotion, even when things don't go your way.'[4]

Mary flared up at once. 'I don't even know the prince. How can I love him? You don't understand

---

[4] Ephesians 5:22

how hard it's all has been,' she finished with tears in her voice.

Dr Hooper's face softened. 'I know it hasn't been easy. God has asked a difficult thing of you, but love is not just a feeling. Love is a choice, a decision of your heart. Ask God for the resolve to love and respect your husband and he will give it to you. And I will pray for you too.'

Mary fumbled for a handkerchief to blow her nose and dab away more stray tears. 'I will try, to please God,' Mary replied emphasising the last part.

'Pleasing your husband might bring you happiness too,' Dr Hooper suggested with a smile. 'But yes, we should want to please God in everything we do. And he promises us blessing when we obey him.'

Empty Arms
(1677-1678)

Mary was angry with Dr Hooper after the interview. She went to evening prayer in her small chapel with a rebellious heart and her prayers ended with a demand that God make William love her. To temper her angry request she meekly promised God that she would love William back. Then she went to bed determined to wait for God to change her husband.

Once Mary had recovered from the journey, William took her on a tour of his palace. It was full of beautiful paintings and furniture that Mary discovered William himself had chosen. He was more relaxed in his own home and he even managed to smile a little when she admired the gardens. It was too cold to explore them fully, but from the short walk they took, she admired the layout and statues.

But they had little time to be alone together. The following week they were off to a state function in The Hague at the grim grey stone Binnenhof Palace where all the important aristocracy and the States General officials gathered. The welcome into the city was exciting with a thirty-one gun salute and a choir of girls singing and spreading orange blossoms on the street. People cheered them from the city gates to the palace grounds. Mary loved the excitement and waved and smiled, but William had turned back into the cold, remote person he was in England. He stood stiffly by her side in the palace as Mary discovered just how much she had to learn about Dutch customs. William whispered instructions to her about whom she should greet with a kiss, who should kiss her and who should just be acknowledged with a smile. Not knowing the language made it even more confusing. But Mary found the people friendly and warm. William, on the other hand, only relaxed when speaking with his aide, Bentinck, or to his army officers. It was an exhausting two days and both of them were glad to return to Honselaerskijck Palace.

As the weeks went by, William's aide and closest friend, Bentinck, began to visit Mary's apartments frequently. He said he was coming to check that the princess was settling in well and not in need of anything. But more often than not, he would spend the evening sitting with Anne Villiers, laughing and talking with her. Mary began to feel a little jealous and lonely. Then she had an idea.

When Bentinck arrived one evening to inquire if everything was to Mary's liking, she replied, 'No.'

A curious silence fell on the room as everyone tried to keep busy but still hear the conversation.

Bentinck's long face was full of concern. 'What may I do for Your Highness?'

'Tell Prince William that I would like to see him too, when you come to visit. We see too little of him here.'

Bentinck smiled and bowed deeply. 'I will inform His Highness of your request. He has many government papers to deal with, but I'm sure he would enjoy visiting here as much as I do.'

Some of the ladies giggled until Mary looked over at them. 'Thank you,' she said primly.

The next day a servant was sent with word that the prince would accompany Bentinck that evening, so Mary began preparations. She told her cook to prepare a warm supper and instructed her ladies to change their habit of complaining about the Dutch, the palace or anything else. Mary looked at Mam in particular when she said this. And finally she chose a gown in the Dutch style. The layered gown had a blue and gold brocade underskirt and a deep blue overskirt with a wide lace collar and cuffs. As she twirled before the long mirror, she was pleased with the effect.

William and Bentinck arrived to find Mary and her ladies occupied with sewing. The servants had already set a table for the supper, which they all sat down to enjoy. Afterwards the table was cleared and some of the ladies began a card game while Anne and Bentinck headed for their favourite window seat. William and Mary stood a little awkwardly until she invited him to sit by the fire with her. Once they were settled, Mary began her planned conversation.

'Were you very busy today?' she inquired.

William sighed. 'More papers, more meetings, too many.'

'Well then, we won't talk about them,' Mary replied. 'Instead let me tell you about my day. I went for a walk in the gardens. They're lovely, although not much is blooming yet. The layout is very charming. You have a very good head gardener I think.'

William leaned back and grinned. 'Do you really like them? I planned the gardens myself. I, or rather we, have an excellent staff of gardeners. I'll have to introduce you to them.'

Mary very quickly realised she had happened on a passionate subject of William's and they had no difficulty filling the evening with talk. And very soon it became a habit. William and Bentinck began to arrive three times a week for a light supper and a relaxing evening of talk, card games or some music. Mary discovered all sorts of things about her new husband. Not only did he design gardens in his spare time, but he was also interested in architecture and collecting works of art. William also loved his army life and he spoke warmly of his men, how they worked together as a team from the commanders down to the foot soldiers. And then there was his passion for hunting, riding through the forests in pursuit of deer or wild boar.

Slowly, a very different picture of William was emerging and Mary couldn't have been more pleased. He was still awkward about the romantic niceties. He didn't remember to bring her flowers like Bentinck did for Anne, but he did smile every time he saw her and was interested to know what she thought and did. So when William announced in the spring of 1678 that he was leaving shortly to join his army on the French border, Mary burst into tears.

'You can't go,' she declared. 'It's too dangerous for the Stadtholder to go. What if you are injured or worse? Who would rule the Netherlands? And what would I do without my husband?'

William hugged her and whispered into her ear, 'You mustn't worry. Pray for me and my men. We'll be in God's hands. As Stadtholder I must defend my country. You, as my wife and Princess of Orange, must also do your duty and submit to God's will.' He hesitated a moment and then whispered, 'And remember, you are *Mijn geliefde vrouw (my beloved wife)*.'

Mary's heart soared. God had answered her prayer.

* * *

The army was scheduled to assemble at Rotterdam a few weeks later, but before William and Bentinck left to join them, Bentinck asked permission to marry Anne Villiers. Both William and Mary happily gave their consent and the two were married two days later. The couple spent their short time together at Bentinck's home in Zorgvliet, a gift from William.

Meanwhile, Mary had some news for William as they sat in her bedroom one evening. The fire warmed the cold spring evening as they sat nestled into an oversized chair. William brushed Mary's deep auburn hair away from her forehead as she leaned against his shoulder. She sighed contentedly.

'I wish you didn't need to leave,' she murmured.

William stiffened slightly, but kept his tone soft. 'You know I must. Please don't go on about it.'

'I won't,' she promised. 'I think I have some special news.' Mary raised her head and looked him in the eye. 'I think I might be pregnant. I'm not sure yet because it is so early ...'

William hugged her fiercely. 'That's wonderful. I will engage Dr Senaer, the best doctor we have, to care for you and our baby. God has truly been good to us.'

For the rest of the evening, no matter what they discussed their eyes would meet and they would think of the baby. William would smile and tenderly hold Mary close.

* * *

After William and Bentinck had been gone a month, Mary was restless and moped about the palace. She kept her usual routine of attending morning and evening prayer services that Dr Hooper led in her private chapel. She wrote letters to friends and her family, rather long sad ones about how much she missed William. And she tried to keep peace between her ladies and the Dutch noble women who came to visit. Mary knew how much William disliked most of her ladies because of their critical, complaining ways and he would be happy to send them all back to England. But Mary knew that would never do because the families of the women, and

King Charles himself, would take it as a personal insult. It was a tiring way to spend the day. Eventually she had enough.

'Anne, let's go find our husbands,' Mary announced one morning after breaking their fast.

Anne was puzzled. 'They're on the battlefield, near Breda, according to the last letter Bentinck wrote me. We can't go there.'

'Not to the battle, no. But William has a palace in Breda. Why can't we go there and be close by? They'll be so surprised to see us.'

'But what about your baby?' Anne asked. 'Would it be safe to travel that far?'

'I'm perfectly well,' Mary insisted.

So the plan was made and a few days later the two women, several servants and luggage were loaded in carriages for the journey. This was the first time that Mary had travelled in this area of the Netherlands. The land was flat and criss-crossed with canals and flat-bottomed boats transporting goods and people. Spring was bringing out some delicate blossoms and flowers that brightened the landscape. The roads, however, were rutted and bumpy and, with no springs in the carriages, it was a rough ride. By the time they arrived at the red brick three-storey palace, they were sore and tired.

The steward greeted them anxiously, having been given little notice of their coming. He tried to address Mary in broken English, but she surprised him with her almost fluent Dutch. She had found it easy to pick up the language during her visits with some of the Dutch noblewomen and as she listened to the Dutch servants. Once rooms had been prepared for them, Mary found she was very tired and lay down on the tester bed. As she drifted off, she suggested that Anne ask the steward to send a message to William and Bentinck.

Several hours later, Mary awoke to hear William's voice in the outer room. She rose eagerly, happy he had been able to come to her so quickly. But as he entered her room Mary fell back into the bed, doubled up with sudden pain.

'Oh, William! Help me!' she gasped as a second wave of agony began to build again.

In the mist of her misery, Mary heard William giving sharp orders and felt hands helping her settle back into the bed. The night was long and full of pain. Mary, certain she was dying, prayed desperately, pleading for God's help. At some point she fell asleep.

The next day she awoke to find William asleep in a chair at her bedside. He was still in his uniform and looked worn out. Mary suddenly felt very sorry she had planned this visit. She tried to sit up, but pain once more tore through her from her hips to her feet. She moaned and William snapped awake.

'Mary, are you all right?' he asked as he moved closer to the bed. But he seemed afraid to touch her, so he called out to Anne to come quickly.

Anne and a strange man entered. Anne hovered at the bottom of the bed, while the stranger came closer, touching her forehead and examining her arms. That was when Mary first noticed the bandages on her arms.

'Seems the bleeding helped, Your Highness,' he said to William. 'The princess should begin to recover now. Although it could take some time before she can travel.'

Mary looked fearfully from the doctor to William. What had happened to her that she needed to be bled and why was she still in so much pain? She waited for them to speak.

William nodded tiredly to the doctor who cleared his throat uncomfortably. 'Your Highness, I regret to inform you that you have lost your baby. You were very ill and will need time to recover, but you are also young and will surely have more children.'

Mary stared at the doctor, not quite taking in what he had said. Then the memory of her stepmother crying, suddenly leapt into her head. Mary Beatrice was young too. She'd had many pregnancies, but no living children. Some had died before they were even born and others died as infants. Would it be the same for her? Tears began to leak out of her eyes as she turned to William.

'I'm sorry,' she said softly. 'I should never have travelled from home. I was so lonely without you. And now our baby is gone.'

William reached over and awkwardly gathered her in his arms, murmuring softly to her. 'Never mind. This was God's will and we must accept it. Perhaps next year, when you are well again …' and his voice cracked with emotion. He held her more tightly.

When William let her go from the embrace, they discovered they were alone in the room. He stood up, straightening his creased uniform and said, 'You must do exactly what the doctor tells you. And you may only travel when he says. Not before. But I do want you back at Honselaerskijck as soon as possible.' He reached over to pick up his discarded overcoat that lay on another chair and threw it over his arm.

Mary watched with rising panic. 'Are you leaving?'

'I must. I've already been away from the battlefield too long.'

'Aren't I more important than your army?' she demanded.

William replied sharply, 'They are your army too, Madam, and they are risking their lives to defend our borders. Don't you realise how close the French are to invading us? Do you want to be imprisoned and your people subjugated to a cruel king who will force them to renounce their faith and become Catholic? I must go. You are in good hands here and I will send word to you as often as I can.'

Mary watched him leave the room feeling more abandoned now than when she first learned she had to leave England.

Finding a New Purpose

(1678-84)

Several weeks later, sixteen-year-old Mary returned to Honselersdijk Palace, weak and still suffering pain in her hips. Two servants, one on each side, helped her up the palace stairs to her apartments and through to her bedchamber. From there, Anne and Mam readied her for bed. Mary lay passively as Mam tucked the covers around her and clucked like a mother hen.

'Filthy Dutch doctors. It's their fault you lost your baby. You need to send for a proper English doctor,' Mam muttered.

Anne, who had just finished instructing the maid to build up the fire to keep Mary warm, replied, 'The prince has already chosen a doctor for the princess. He is supposed to be the best in all of Europe in caring for women's illnesses.'

Mam made a rude noise and continued fussing.

Mary didn't care, not even when the new doctor came to examine her. She endured the poking and prodding without complaint and merely nodded or shook her head to his questions. When he had finished he looked very serious.

'Your Highness, I'm sorry I was not with you when this tragedy struck. I believe you should have had better care.' Mam made a triumphant noise in the background. 'You will need a considerable time to recover and you must follow my instructions closely. I will explain all to your ladies.'

Mary turned her head away. Her baby was gone. She didn't care about anything else.

* * *

Mary did recover slowly and so did her spirits. By the time the trees began to lose their leaves, she was able to walk about the gardens with her ladies. Best of all, William was returning from the battlefield, having kept the French army from breaking through the Netherlands' borders.

It was a joyous reunion and several months later, both Mary and Anne knew they were pregnant. They spent many happy hours sewing baby clothes and discussing nursemaids and routines. Then disaster struck.

Anne's pregnancy progressed well and she gave birth to a healthy girl. But that same spring of 1679, Mary became very ill again and Dr Senaer ordered her to bed where she spent the next three months lost in a mist of fevers and pain. In the end, the doctor sadly informed both William and Mary that Mary would have no children.

'You have been plagued with infections in your body, Your Highness,' he explained to Mary as she lay in her bed. 'It is no longer possible for you to conceive a child.'

William leapt up from his chair by the side of the bed. 'Is this certain?' he asked, casting an anxious look at his wife.

Dr Senaer replied, 'Nothing is impossible for God, but from my experience I must tell you not to expect to have any children. I'm very sorry.'

Mary said nothing. She couldn't. Her mouth refused to work. She couldn't even cry. She just felt numb. She turned her face away from the doctor and William and closed her eyes. She just wanted everyone to go away and leave her alone.

* * *

For the next two months, Mary lay in bed, refusing to get up and eating only enough to stop Mam from nagging her. William came to sit with her when he could get away from his pile of government papers and council meetings. But he had little to say and, after a while, became impatient with Mary and her refusal to try to get on with her life. He usually left with a brisk 'goodnight' and no kiss for her. Mary was sure he had fallen out of love with her and she would weep into her pillow afterwards.

Dr Hooper, however, was more persistent. He arrived every morning to read the Scriptures to her. Mary had refused to get out of bed even for the morning and evening prayer services, so Dr Hooper brought them to her. She found him very annoying, and tried to block out his kindly meant reminders of God's sovereignty. Her sadness and lethargy only grew deeper and deeper. But Dr Hooper refused to give up. So Mary would pretend to go to sleep as soon as he began to settle his round body in the armchair that Anne provided for him. In spite of that he cleared his throat, rustling the pages of the Bible looking for the day's reading.

> Hear my prayer, O LORD; let my cry come to you! Do not hide your face from me in the day of my distress!
>
> Incline your ear to me; answer me speedily in the day when I call! For my days pass away like smoke, and my bones burn like a furnace.
>
> My heart is struck down like grass and has withered; I forget to eat my bread. Because of my loud groaning my bones cling to my flesh.
>
> I am like a desert owl of the wilderness, like an owl of the waste places; I lie awake; I am like a lonely sparrow on the housetop. [5]

'That's how I feel, like that lonely sparrow,' Mary interrupted. 'Why has God forsaken me?'

'He hasn't, Your Highness,' Dr Hooper assured her. 'The psalmist knew all about suffering, but he always knew that God was near him. Listen,' he urged as he flipped back a few pages.

> O LORD my God, I cried to you for help, and you have healed me. O LORD, you have brought up my soul from Sheol; you restored me to life from

---

[5] Psalm 102:1-7

among those who go down to the pit.
Sing praises to the LORD, O you his saints, and give
thanks to his holy name. For his anger is but for a
moment, and his favour is for a lifetime.

Weeping may tarry for the night, but joy comes
with the morning. [6]

'God will rescue you from your distress and bring joy
to you once more,' Dr Hooper explained.

'But will he give me children?' Mary demanded.

Dr Hooper drew his bushy eyebrows down in
concentration. 'Surely Your Highness wouldn't bargain
with the Almighty God?' he asked. 'God does all things for
his good purpose as St Paul tells us in Romans, even our
afflictions. We might not see his purpose at the time, but
God has promised to work out everything to his glory.'

'But I want children,' Mary wailed. 'Is that wrong?'

Dr Hooper sighed heavily and took her hand.
'Your Highness desires a good thing, but we are God's
creatures. Should the creature tell the creator how to
ordain events? I don't know why God has refused you
children, but I do know that we are placed on this
earth to serve him, not for him to serve us.'

Mary jerked her hand away from her chaplain and
struggled to sit up. Mam rushed forward to help her,
but Mary told her sharply to go away. Looking back
at Dr Hooper, Mary demanded, 'So God expects me
to gladly obey him even though he takes away the one
thing I need and want.'

---

[6] Psalm 30:2-5

'Need?' Dr Hooper challenged.

'Yes. I'm a princess who must produce an heir for William, a son to inherit. I need to have children.'

Dr Hooper replied, 'And you think God doesn't know that?' He paused long enough to take a deep breath. 'Excuse my bluntness, Your Highness, but you may not hide in your bed feeling sorry for yourself. You may not demand from God what you think will make you happy. God is in control, not you.'

Mary stared at her chaplain and then flopped back onto her pillows. 'Go away. I don't want to hear any more.' She turned her head away and closed her eyes.

After a while she heard everyone leave the bedchamber and she was alone with her thoughts. She was angry and full of self-pity.

'All my life I've had to obey others,' she complained to God. 'First my uncle, the king, takes me away from my father. Then my father tells me who I must marry. My husband takes me to a foreign land, away from my family. And now you, God, have told me I may not have children! Where is your goodness?'

As she lay there, thinking her angry thoughts, suddenly the words from the Lord's Prayer came into her mind. 'Your will be done on earth as it is in heaven.'[7] She had prayed those words many times. But had she really meant them?

---

[7] Matthew 6:10

'Is this really your will?' she asked God. 'Why does it have to be so difficult?'

Then words from Jesus' prayer in Gethsemane echoed in her thoughts. 'My Father, if it be possible, let this cup pass from me; nevertheless, not as I will, but as you will.'[8] Even Jesus, God's own Son, had found his Father's will difficult.

'But I don't want this! I don't like your will!' she complained. And then overwhelmed, she gave up her fight and prayed, 'Help me! Please Heavenly Father, help me in my distress.'

Suddenly, very tired, Mary could feel herself drifting into sleep. As she did, she felt her anger begin to drain away, replaced by a warm peace.

* * *

Mary's recovery continued to be a slow process. As April turned to May she still struggled with fevers and weakness as well as depression, but instead of being angry with Dr Hooper's visits she began to look forward to them. She was eager to hear God's Word; it gave her the hope she so desperately longed for.

William came to visit her too, but his stays remained short and his manner brisk. Mary was sure he blamed her for her childlessness and her weakness.

Finally, she was able to get out of bed and take short walks in the large garden full of summer blooms. She usually rested in the Orangery, a glass house William had built in the garden. It was full of exotic plants and

---

[8] Matthew 26:39

trees from around the world and caged song birds. Mary found herself refreshed after time spent listening to the birds and enjoying the citrus and jasmine fragrances.

It was here that Mary first met Baroness Van Arnhem. William had urged her to meet the stately matron and, after growing weary of William's insistence, she finally gave in. Anne, who was once more expecting a child, and several of her other ladies had joined them in the Orangery. The servants brought tea and poffertjes for everyone to enjoy.

'Your Highness,' the baroness began as she settled her substantial person into a large chair. She wore a deep black velvet gown. 'How wonderful to see you recovering your strength. The entire country has been very concerned. Prayers are offered up in all the churches each Sunday.'

Mary smiled and nodded.

Taking that as encouragement, the baroness continued. 'The prince has asked me to tell you about the work that I do and ask if you might join me.'

Mary bit her tongue. She almost made a tart comment about being told yet again what to do. Instead, she nodded for the baroness to continue.

'With my family all grown, I have much time on my hands and more money than I know what to do with. God has blessed our family well. So I now use my time and money to do charity work. I have organised sewing circles to provide clothing for the poor, especially the children. And we care for orphans too. We supply money for orphanages so the children have a safe place to live, provide training for jobs for the young men, and seek to find suitable husbands for the young ladies. Your patronage would mean a great deal to the children.'

Mary's heart melted as the baroness went on to tell her the sad stories of some of the orphans. With no parents to care for them, they lived on the streets until someone is willing to take them in. After hearing this Mary couldn't sit in her comfortable palace. She resolved to help them.

Even though she still wasn't physically strong, Mary could still organise her ladies to begin a sewing circle of their own. They had to devote at least two hours each day, except the Sabbath, to sewing simple gowns, shirts, breeches and small clothing. The ladies grumbled, but Mary ignored their complaints and joined them whenever she could. Meanwhile, she also spent a short time each day seated at her desk, writing to friends to urge them to help also. As the months wore on and Mary improved, she also began to visit the orphanages, delivering the clothes she and her ladies had made. She treated each child kindly, knowing they needed love as much as they needed food and clothing. If God would not give her children of her own, then she would care for those who had no parents.

* * *

The following year, in 1684, Mary discovered another cause she could not ignore. Feeling healthier than she had since she was first pregnant six years ago, she began to take an interest in events in the country. William was still away with the army far more than he was at home and Mary tried not to mind. She had accepted that as Stadtholder he was required to defend the country. She tried not to worry about him being injured or even killed, and prayed daily for peace. As a result of the ongoing war with France, refugees came pouring over the borders daily. French Protestants were fleeing their country as the king and Catholic church began to persecute them in earnest. Some of the stories that filtered into Mary's court circle horrified her and she decided to investigate the truth of the matter.

Mary's request for more information brought the Marquis de Venours to Honselersdijk Palace in the company of Baroness Van Arnhem. They were both shown into Mary's study and a servant brought a tray of hot chocolate and peperkoek.

The stout baroness looked even larger next to the short thin marquis. Mary judged him to be about fifty as he bowed deeply to her. His clothes had once been elegant but, although clean, were now shabby after long wear. Together they sat by the fire and sipped their chocolate while Mary, speaking in French, began to question him. The marquis answered calmly between bites of his cake. Except for the scars on his face and hands, he didn't look like someone who was under death threats from the French government.

'I'm very grateful, Your Highness, that you and the prince have welcomed my people into your country. The persecution is terrible and many have lost their lives rather than give up their faith. Even when the French army has herded large groups into churches, demanding they recant their Protestant beliefs or die, they stand firm. My daughters and I are very fortunate to have escaped.'

Mary left her hot chocolate cooling as the marquis recounted story after story of the tortures and executions. Finally she could hear no more.

'Please tell me what I can do to help these people,' she interrupted.

The marquis replied. 'My biggest concern is for the women refugees. Their husbands and fathers have either been imprisoned or killed and they have no one to protect them, even in this country that allows them to worship according to the true faith.'

Baroness Van Arnhem chimed in. 'The marquis has already set up a home in Haarlem where women can live together safely. Many of the Haarlem people have given generously to help them. But more houses are needed, especially here.'

Mary was silent for a moment, thinking of the plight of those women coming to a new country with nothing but what they could carry and no family to help them. These women needed help just as much as the orphans, and Mary knew she could provide what was needed.

'Where do we begin?' she asked. 'How many houses do you need and how much money?'

As the marquis outlined his plans for more homes Mary nodded eagerly and promised much. She only hoped that William would approve.

Political Interruptions

(1684-1685)

Mary decided to speak to William as soon as he returned from Amsterdam and his meeting with the States-General. She sent him an invitation to join her that evening for a light supper in her apartments. He came with a gloomy face and a tired slump in his shoulders.

'Did the States-General not go well?' Mary asked as they sat down at the table and the servants began to serve the meal.

'A disaster,' William declared, nodding to the servant who offered him soup from a large tureen. 'Those old men are too cautious and too concerned with protecting their fortunes. They'd rather sign peace treaties so they can keep up their trade with the Far East.' He became passionate as he demanded. 'Why not just give France our land on a silver platter while they're at it? Who cares that many gallant soldiers have given their lives to defend our borders from the French army!' He slammed his fist on the table causing both their soup bowls to rock and spill on the white linen cloth.

Mary waved away the startled servants who left the dining room quickly. Mary suddenly felt sorry for William. He looked so tired, more tired and discouraged than she had seen him in some time. But since he had always refused to discuss politics with her in the past, she knew it was useless for her to ask him any questions now. So she changed the subject immediately.

As she took her napkin and began mopping up the soup, she said cheerfully, 'I've been making plans while you've been away.'

'Plans? About what?' he asked, also mopping up his own soup.

'I have a house plan I want to show you.'

'A house? Haven't I given you enough houses? Do you need more?' William was puzzled.

Mary laughed. 'No, no, not for me. A house for Huguenot women, just outside The Hague. I've bought the property already and I've had plans drawn up by an architect.'

Together they went to her study, the meal forgotten. Mary showed him the plans and told him about her visit with Marquis de Venours. 'Those women need someone to help them,' Mary finished.

William studied the plans further before looking up at her with a smile. 'You have done well,' he said. 'We must do all we can for the Huguenot refugees. That's one reason I fight the French so vigorously.'

'Then you don't mind the expense?' Mary asked as she sat down by the fireplace.

William joined her, touching her hair softly with his fingers. 'Of course not! Haven't I always told you that wherever you find a good cause, we should give what we can?' He settled himself into the deep chair, pushing aside his long curly hair from his face. 'I dislike intolerance of any kind, but especially when it comes to our faith. Our Lord never told us to persecute anyone who didn't believe. Pray for them, yes, preach to them, of course, but do not threaten them with torture or death. I've met some of the Huguenots myself and each time it angers me more and spurs me on to want to repel the French from our borders.'

Mary realised they had strayed into politics once more and she didn't want William upset all over again. So she plunged in with the next thing that came to her mind.

'I went to visit Anne a few days ago to see her new baby. She's asked us to be godparents.'

William smiled. 'Bentinck mentioned that to me too. They have quite a brood now. It's four, isn't it?'

'Yes, I saw them all. Henry is so touchingly serious, but Mary and Anne laughed and played with me. They plan to name the newest one Frances, after Anne's mother.' Then suddenly Mary asked a question she had always been afraid to ask.

'William, do you blame me because we can't have children?'

He sat up with a start, confused at the sudden change of topic. 'What? Why would I blame you when it's God who decides these matters?'

Mary couldn't look at him, so she studied her hands instead.

William reached over to her and drew her into his arms. 'Have you been worrying about this all these years? There was no need. I wish fervently that we did have children, but if God has ordained otherwise we must be content.'

Mary sank into his embrace with relief. 'Then you still care for me?'

'*Mijn geliefde vrouw*, you can be very foolish,' he replied with a deep sigh as he held her tight. 'I have never stopped loving you even though I can't always be here. We're not like an ordinary couple who can sit at home each night by the fire. I wish it were so, but our position means we are here to serve others. You know I must put my people first and you must do the same. I lead the army and deal with the grumpy old men in Amsterdam, and others like our uncle, King Charles. But that's another matter. And you must be like a mother to our people, helping the widows and orphans and any others who cannot help themselves. But none of this needs to mean we no longer care for one another. Surely you know that.'

Mary's only answer was to hug William tightly and kiss him. He returned her kisses, murmuring once more *Mijn geliefde vrouw*.

* * *

By autumn of 1684, the house for the Huguenot women was completed and Mary was invited to tour it and meet the new occupants. Dressed in a gown, shoes and cloak much plainer than she normally wore, she boarded her carriage with several of her Dutch ladies-in-waiting. Mary knew her English women, with the exception of Anne, would only make offensive comments if she brought them along.

Mary was greeted by Mademoiselle Obdam, the newly appointed director of the home. The middle-aged woman led Mary through the small formal garden, pointing out the chapel at the back of the property and the gardener's small cottage nearby. As they entered the large sitting room about a dozen women suddenly stood up, leaving their sewing or books aside. The women were from all stations in life and of various ages, but Mary saw immediately the one thing they had in common. Most of them had been disfigured by torture in some way and they all had deep grief etched on their faces.

Twenty-one-year-old Mary couldn't speak for a moment, afraid she would burst into tears in front of them. These women had suffered terribly and Mary felt ashamed. She had been angry with God because he had denied her children and she had been angry at one time and another with her father, her uncle and even William, who gave her no choices of her own. She thought she had suffered more than anyone else. But here were women who had suffered far more. They had endured torture, lost their husbands or fathers and had to run for their very lives. Mary's complaints seemed rather small next to these women. Forgive me, she prayed silently. Almighty God, please help me to be thankful for what I have.

Mary then met each woman and heard a little of their stories. She toured the rest of the house, seeing each of the bedrooms, the kitchen and ending in the large dining hall where she shared a light supper with the women. She came away with a renewed sense of urgency to help as many of these women as she could.

* * *

Mary spent the rest of that year immersed in her charity work. When she wasn't visiting orphanages and refuge homes, she was sewing right along with her ladies or writing letters to encourage others to help. She did take time out to visit Anne and her children. Bentinck, who always accompanied William to the army or on state business, left Anne alone as much as William left her. Mary enjoyed the chance to play with the children and just chat with her friend.

Mary also kept up a long correspondence with her sister and stepmother, getting all the news from England. Her sister was particularly good at letting Mary know the latest gossip. Since her marriage to Prince George of Denmark two years before, Anne had lost two babies. So her letters were full of sadness too. Her father wrote her on occasion, sometimes scolding her for not forcing William to do what King Charles wanted him to do on matters of trade and alliances. Mary would shake her head when she read those letters. How could anyone possibly expect her to tell William what to do? Besides, she had to be loyal to her husband as God had commanded. Mary thought her father was being very unfair to even ask her. Then suddenly all her nicely ordered life began to change.

After the Christmas season, Dr Ken, Mary's new chaplain, had announced that the Lord's Supper would be celebrated the following Sabbath. Mary, as had become her custom, cancelled her social engagements and retired to her study each evening to read the Bible and pray in preparation. Then, one evening, a servant interrupted her devotions to say the prince requested that she come to his audience chamber. Surprised, Mary obeyed. Normally William didn't interfere with her devotions, although he might have been too busy to remember.

When she arrived, she saw their cousin, the Duke of Monmouth, standing by the fireplace. Mary laughed at his exaggerated courtly bow and gave him a warm hug and kiss. Monmouth hadn't changed much over the years; he was still as handsome and confident as ever.

William watched with an amused smile. 'Our cousin has been sent out of England and has come to us for refuge. Shall we let him stay?'

'Oh, yes!' Mary replied. 'I'd love to hear news from England first hand.'

Monmouth shook his head mournfully, although not with much seriousness. 'Suspicion and distrust are everywhere in England. Even my own father suspects me of treason. I've been shoved out of the nest to fend for myself.'

'Now, now,' William interrupted. 'Let's get the facts straight. I believe there was a plot against your father, the king, but he can hardly have thought you were involved or you'd be in prison instead of standing in front of my fireplace.'

'True, true, cousin. But my father did have to banish me to keep the Duke of York happy. I'm sorry, Mary, but your father is not my favourite person.'

William shook his head and replied good-naturedly, 'Well then, cousin, we will have to put up with you. I'll have an apartment at the Mauritshuis in The Hague prepared for you. You may stay as long as you like.'

And so it was settled. Thirty-six-year-old Monmouth left promising to return the next day to take Mary on a walk through the parks. William caught Mary's eye and silenced her protests until Monmouth had left for the evening.

'William, I can't possibly take the time to be tour guide to our cousin. You know how many things I must do.'

'Yes, I know, but this is important. We need to keep Monmouth occupied so he'll stay a while.'

Puzzled, Mary wanted to know why.

'As our uncle, King Charles, grows older, people are thinking about who the next king will be. Charles has no legitimate children and since Monmouth is only a child by one of his mistresses, he can't inherit the throne. So the next choice is your father. I don't like your father and neither do the English people. He's a Catholic and not a wise man. However, that is the way the succession should be and I will support him. But Monmouth would like to be king himself and some influential people have promised to help him, to make him think he can do it. So we have to keep him out of England and away from those people, or he will cause civil war in England once more.'

Mary was amazed that William was actually discussing politics with her. And pleased too. She would do all she could to help. So the next day, and for many days after that, Mary kept up an exhausting schedule of activities. She took Monmouth on a tour of the ice sculptures in The Hague. They went skating on the frozen canals and he even tried to play *kloven* with some of the local young men. William suggested a ball, so Mary planned an extravagant evening at their House in the Woods and invited all the aristocracy. By the end of January 1685 Mary was exhausted and gladly let William take Monmouth off to their hunting lodge in Dierns for a few weeks.

All went according to plan, until the dreadful news arrived a few weeks later. King Charles had died of a stroke and the Duke of York had been proclaimed King James II, and Mary the Heir Apparent. Monmouth was furious and he packed his bags immediately. He promised Mary he wouldn't go to England, but he lied. By June, the whole sorry story emerged and Mary was in tears when she heard it told.

William received letters while they were at their Het Loo Palace supervising some of the renovations to the building and gardens. It was the first time in a long while Mary had had William all to herself. But the letters brought it all to a halt.

'We must leave immediately for The Hague,' William explained. 'Our cousin, Monmouth, has led a rebellion against your father and has lost. Your father has ordered all of the rebels hung and another 1200 deported.'

'What about Monmouth?' Mary asked fearfully.

William was grim as he scanned the rest of the letter. 'He's dead, beheaded for treason.'

Mary gasped. 'How could my father be so cruel?'

William shrugged. 'It was poorly done. Very unwise. The English people are already anxious about having a Catholic king and now he has had so many killed in revenge that the people are becoming angry. But you must write your father straightaway and tell him we had nothing to do with this, because I'm sure he will blame us.'

Defending the Faith

(1685–88)

Mary wrote to her father, as William had advised her to do, assuring the king that she and William had not had any part in Monmouth's plans. King James replied that he accepted her explanation, but her letter also prompted an unexpected response several months later.

Mary had just returned from visiting Anne Bentinck, who was mourning the loss of her fifth and youngest child. They had wept together and prayed together. Mary was in no mood to receive an unannounced guest. As she entered her audience chamber, a man suddenly rose from a chair and bowed down on one knee to her, as was proper now that she was Heir Apparent. Surprised, Mary stopped abruptly and stared at him. He was garishly dressed in an orange satin overcoat trimmed with ribbons and buttons and a red velvet vest and breeches. His long brown wig obscured his face until he straightened up and then she saw his satisfied smile.

'Who are you?' she demanded, irritated and a little alarmed. 'How did you get in here?'

'Your Highness, I am the Marquis d'Albeville.' the man responded with a pronounced Irish accent. 'Your father, King James, sent me with special letters and instructions for your ears only.'

'Indeed,' Mary responded coldly. 'You will have to wait until my receiving hours this afternoon.'

Unconcerned by the dismissal, the marquis carried on, 'Your Highness, these are personal matters. Private things that the king wishes me to present to you as soon as possible. I'm sure you would not wish to keep me waiting to carry out my duty.'

Shocked at his arrogance, Mary replied, 'How dare you come into my apartments unannounced! Being sent by the King of England does not give you free access to me or my court. You will leave at once!'

The marquis's eyes widened in surprise. Belatedly, several servants rushed into the room. They hastily bowed to Mary and, with apologies, hustled the unresisting marquis toward the door. Over his shoulder he called out, 'I will return this afternoon, Your Highness.'

Mary found that she was trembling and sat down in a nearby chair. She felt chilled to think that someone was able to get by her servants and the palace guard. She would have to speak sharply to the steward and William was sure to get angry when he heard about it. Meanwhile, her ladies also entered the room and clustered around her anxiously.

'I'm unhurt,' she assured them. 'Please don't fuss.'

The Marquis d'Albeville returned the following day during her receiving hours. Mary was tempted to turn him away even though he had an appointment, but then she thought better of it. Instead she kept him waiting while she drew out her visit with several Dutch baronesses who had come to pay a social call. At last, Mary nodded to the soldier who now stood guard inside her audience chamber to show the marquis into her study.

Resisting the temptation to make the irritating man stand throughout the interview, Mary nodded to a chair opposite her small mauve and yellow settee.

Settling himself down, he began, 'Your Highness, King James has entrusted me with an errand close to his heart. He is most concerned for the spiritual welfare of his daughters and he has sent with me letters and books that he wants you to read so that you might better understand the Catholic religion.'

Surprised, Mary asked, 'Were you sent to my sister too?'

'No, Your Highness. The king spoke to her himself since she lives in London. But,' he paused for effect, 'he appointed me his spokesman to you. Since both of you were so incorrectly taught in your childhood, the king wishes now to give you a chance to understand the true faith. He dearly hopes that you will see the light as he has and convert to Catholicism. I've been sent to answer any questions about anything you don't yet understand. Although,' he added reluctantly, 'the king also sent Father Morgan, a Jesuit priest, to give instruction as well.'

Mary felt anger rise in her. Did this man really think she could so easily reject her faith? She replied stiffly, 'Thank you for delivering the letters and books. Please leave them on my desk. You may tell my father I appreciate his concern for me and that I will read what he has sent me. Do not interrupt me!' she said as the marquis opened his mouth to speak. 'I don't need you or Father Morgan to give me spiritual instruction. I have my own chaplain. Tell the king I will write him directly and answer his questions concerning my faith.'

'But, Your Highness, it is the king's wish that you use me and Father Morgan as a resource. And,' he added with a touch of conspiracy, 'if you convert to Catholicism then you will be assured of the crown after your father. But if you do not and your sister does convert ...'

Mary had had enough. 'Get out!' she ordered.

The marquis realised he had gone too far and began to apologise, but Mary refused to listen. She rose and turned her back on him until he bowed and left her study.

Staring out the window onto the summer garden, Mary began to pray quietly. 'Almighty God, please help me. Give me the wisdom I need as I read what my father has sent me that I might know the truth. Give me the words to answer him.' She also prayed for her sister, Anne, that she too would know how to answer their father.

For the rest of 1687, Mary read her father's papers, her mother's confession before she died and even a paper written by her uncle, King Charles, all explaining their conversions of Catholicism. She had been shocked to discover her uncle's deathbed conversion. She also studied the books, making notes as she read. By the end of November, she felt ready to reply. It had taken a long time to work through all the material, partly because she had not studied much over the years and partly because of her eyes. The strain of so much study by candlelight weakened her sight, causing headaches and watery sight. But she persevered and finally felt ready to begin the letter. Giving orders that she was not to be disturbed, Mary began the next day, writing and rewriting until she had down on paper what she hoped was a clear answer to her father.

December 1687

Your Majesty,

Thank you for the letters and books you sent. I have studied them and was gratified to learn how you and my mother came to change your religion. Please know that what I am writing to you is not easy because I do not wish to be disrespectful to my father. But I must speak the truth, so please excuse any offence that I might give.

First, let me say I am not a scholar and would not hope to give you a scholarly debate. Instead, I will simply speak as first I was taught and then came to know for myself from reading the Scriptures. As both our Lord himself and St Paul commanded, we must each 'enquire diligently into the Scriptures,' to know the truth.

You say we must rely on the pope and the church to teach the truth as Jesus himself ordained, but I must disagree. There is no proof in Scripture of the infallibility of the pope or his succession. Many popes in the past have not spoken God's truth nor acted in a Christian manner. You say our salvation rests in our submission to the Catholic church, but I believe my salvation rests in my submission to God and reading his Word to understand how I must live each day. You say that people may not interpret the Bible for themselves, that they have poor understanding of Holy Scripture and make wrong interpretations. But I believe that we have each been created with reason and even the simplest of folk can be given understanding by God to hear his Word and respond to his gospel. I agree that many Protestants don't live as they should, bringing shame instead of glory to God. But, Sire, many Catholics are the same. Our respective religions should be judged by using God's Word as the standard, not the lives of imperfect people.

God has sustained me through my dark hours, giving me the strength to face my difficulties. I could

*not live except that I am given the ability to read his
Word, and seek him in prayer and in the sacraments.
I know in whom I believe and I know he will sustain
me until the end of my days. The gates of hell will not
prevail so long as our Lord himself is with his Church
until the end of time.*[9]

*Your obedient daughter and servant,
Mary*

William approved her letter when she showed it to
him. Feeling encouraged, she folded it carefully,
sealed and handed it to a servant to add it to the
bundle of letters and papers that would be taken by
a trusted courier aboard a ship bound for England.
Also in that bundle were letters to her sister, Anne,
and Dr Compton, Bishop of London. Mary wanted
to encourage her sister to remain strong in her faith
and not give in to any pressure from their father.
And she wanted Dr Compton to know about her
correspondence with the king in case any rumours
started that she might convert to Catholicism.

Mary set down her pen with a great sigh. Her
family, politics and her religion were all tangled up
together. And she had suspected it would only get
worse.

---

[9] This is a summary of the letter Mary wrote to her father at this time.
The entire text (four pages long) can be found in Marjorie Bowen's *The
Third Mary Stuart*, Appendix A, pp. 294-298.

* * *

King James replied to Mary with compliments about how well she wrote her letter, but he was not in the least persuaded. In fact, his letter contained yet more pleas for her to convert and a suggestion that she speak with the Jesuit priest he had sent. And then he sent more papers and books to read.

Mary sat with the bundle in front of her on her desk and then looked up at the frost covered windows. She felt too weary to begin all that study all over again. The marquis was still a pest, turning up most days to inquire how her reading was going. She told him repeatedly she didn't need his help, but he seemed incapable of taking the hint.

I can't keep doing this and letting my other duties go, she thought. I must see to my charities and my duties as William's hostess. And I won't give up my own devotions either. Mary was beginning to suspect some of her father's plan was to distract her from what was most important: her own spiritual life and responsibilities before God. So she decided to continue to read her father's books only when time permitted.

By May of 1688, Mary had written to her father a number of times and then realised they had reached an impasse. He refused to understand the Protestant doctrines and she refused to convert to Catholicism. But then politics raised its ugly head once more.

Mary knew that there was discontent in England with her father's reign. He was insisting on placing

Catholics in all the top government positions, which was against the law. When the parliament refused to change the law, James disbanded the parliament and changed the law himself. Most people were outraged, and some of the dukes and earls were heard to say that Mary would make a better monarch than her father. All the talk unsettled Mary. So much so that she found herself complaining to Dr Burnett, an Englishman who had come to live at the Dutch court after he fell out of favour with King James. He had quickly become a good friend to both William and Mary.

'I like our life here. I wish the English people would realise that I have responsibilities in Holland that I can't leave,' Mary said as she walked in the garden with the older man.

'But your duty, Your Highness. If your people need you ...' he let his sentence trail off.

'I have no experience,' Mary protested. 'I can't rule a whole country. William could, of course, but he can't leave the Netherlands without a Stadtholder. So we can't go.'

Dr Burnett stopped and stared at Mary.

'What's wrong?' Mary asked suddenly even more concerned.

Taking a deep breath, Dr Burnett suggested that they sit in the Orangery for a while. Once they were settled, he began. 'Your Highness, I'm not sure that you understand the situation fully. You are your father's heir to the throne, not your husband. He will not rule in England. It's you that will be called upon to take your father's place. Alone.'

'That can't be!' Mary exclaimed. 'I can't be a queen without my husband. It's against God's law. No, No. A husband is never to be subject to his wife! If I'm ever to be a queen, then William would have to be king.'

'But that's never been done. England has never had joint monarchs to rule over them.' Dr Burnett replied with a deeply worried look on his face.

'Good,' Mary replied with a smile. 'Then I can't be queen.'

Warming Pans and Revolution

(1688-89)

Mary soon discovered that she could not avoid the English crown. In May 1688, just after her 26th birthday, she received a letter from her sister, Princess Anne, describing Queen Mary Beatrice's recent unfriendliness to Anne. Anne and Mary Beatrice were both expecting babies and Anne felt sure they should be closer friends. Mary sighed, wishing they would get along. Mary prayed for their health and their unborn babies, and then ceased to worry about it. But then matters grew much worse.

Anne's next letter, over a month later, reported rumours that Mary Beatrice had delivered her baby early and he had died. Since the birth had been so quick, none of the usual dignitaries had been summoned to witness the birth. Taking advantage of this, it was said that a healthy baby boy had been smuggled into the queen's room in a warming pan and presented as the new heir to the throne! Mary could scarcely believe it. She took the letter immediately to William.

She found him in his study with Bentinck poring over papers on a large desk. She greeted them quickly, sat down and showed them the letter. She finished rather breathlessly, 'Could it really have happened?'

Both men leaned back in their chairs and William held up a letter of his own. 'It seems many people do believe it, including the seven men who wrote this letter.'

Mary was suddenly aware that something even more serious was coming. 'What men?'

'The leading men in England: the Earls Danby, Shrewsbury, and Devonshire, Lord Lumley, Russell, Sidney and the Bishop of London. They're inviting me to bring an army to England to oust your father and make you their queen,' he explained.

Mary was horrified. 'No, no, you can't. The king is my father. How can we take his throne away?'

William nodded. 'I understand your concern, but you and I don't always get to do what we want. Your people are asking for our help. Do we turn our backs on them while your father continues to ignore the laws? Or even possibly substitute a child to take your place and thereby carry on his Catholic rule?'

'No,' Mary replied more quietly, feeling defeated.

Bentinck spoke up. 'The letter assures the prince that the people are ready to receive him and there should be no bloodshed. Your father's army is in disarray and he will run at the first sign of our troops. So you don't need to worry for either the prince's safety or your father's.'

Mary looked helplessly over at William, who stood up and came around to sit on the corner of the desk. He said gently, 'We must do this, and I will go with you every step of the way. We will rule together.'

Mary shook her head. 'Dr Burnett said that can't be.'

William smiled. 'If they want my army, then they must offer us a joint throne. I think that they will suddenly discover that it's possible after all.'

And it was. The day Mary heard that news she took to her bed and wept long and hard. She didn't want to leave her beloved home or her beautiful gardens and especially not the Dutch people. They had been so kind to her over the last eleven years and she now loved them far more than her English subjects.

William prepared his army and navy during the summer with the blessing of the State-General, who voted him extra funds for military use. Mary continued to correspond with her sister, urging her to discover more details around the royal birth. Anne did her best, but could learn little more than she already reported. Neither of them could forget their little stepsister's secret Catholic baptism thirteen years earlier. Could her father and stepmother really have substituted a baby this time?

By October, William was ready to leave for England. He came to her bedchamber to say goodbye. After shooing the servant out, he took her in his arms and kissed her.

As he held her, he began to speak softly, 'This could be a dangerous mission, and I may be killed.'

All the fear and worry bubbled up and she began to cry. Amid the tears she pleaded with him not to go. He waited for her to calm down and then said something even worse.

'Should it be God's will that I die, then you must promise me to remarry. And you must promise to marry a good Protestant, one who loves God and lives to serve him.'

Mary could scarcely believe this conversation. 'I don't want any other husband,' she replied in an anguished whisper.

William held her tenderly, close to tears himself, and wouldn't let her go until she finally promised amid tears and protests. Then he was gone.

The next three months were full of anguish for Mary. She held her breath every time a new bundle of letters arrived and then breathed a happy sigh of relief each time she opened William's handwritten letters. She read of his dangerous voyage across the North Sea, his arrival at the English coastal town of Torbay, and of his long, unopposed march through the south of England to London. All along the way townspeople and farmers had cheered his army on, welcoming him as their deliverer.

Though relieved at William's welcome in England, she still worried about her father's fate. She pleaded with God in prayer to protect him as well as her husband, wrestling with the fifth commandment: Honour your father and your mother. Mary was torn by the fear that she was breaking God's law, even as she was answering her duty to be queen. She spent many hours seeking wisdom and peace from God.

In late November, Mary received an agitated servant from her friend, Anne Bentinck's, household.

'You must come at once, Your Highness,' he said. 'I'm afraid that my mistress' life is coming to a close.'

Mary's heart sank and tears rose to her eyes. She thanked the young man and said she would leave immediately. Mary ordered her warm fur-lined cloak and muff be brought at once and the carriage made ready.

Within the hour, Mary was sitting by her friend's bedside, a fire blazing in the marble fireplace. Worried servants and a tired doctor stood around the bedchamber. Anne, pale and thin, lay still in the sumptuous bed. Mary took her cold hand in hers as Anne opened her eyes and smiled weakly.

Mary squeezed Anne's hand and said, 'My dear, dear friend. What may I do for you?'

'Take care of my children. See that they get safely to their father.'

Tears rolled down Mary's cheeks. 'Yes, of course. When I sail for England, they will be with me in my cabin. And I will deliver them to Bentinck myself.'

Anne smiled and closed her eyes once more. Mary asked one of the servants to bring her a Bible, and she read to her friend comforting words from the Scriptures.

As she finished, the doctor spoke. 'You should allow her children to say goodbye. The time is very near.'

Mary nodded and closed the Bible. 'Bring the children in.'

The five children entered slowly, and starting with the oldest, nine-year-old Mary, they came over to the bed to kiss their mother. Even six-month-old Isabella, held by her nurse, reached out and patted her mother's face. Then Mary gathered them around her and they watched as Anne Bentinck passed quietly away.

* * *

The Christmas season was a sad one that year; consoling grieving children, missing Anne Bentinck, and William too. She went through all her possessions, determining what to take with her and what to give away. She went to the parties and dinners given in her honour in the New Year, tearfully saying goodbye to her Dutch court and friends. Then in February 1689, Mary boarded a ship with Anne Bentinck's children and sailed away from her beloved Holland.

God sent fair weather that provided a quick voyage, and the ship docked at Greenwich the following day. Mary left the ship as dignified as she could, though she longed to fling herself into William's arms. She received all the formal greetings patiently, but her heart quickened as William approached. His face below his wide-brimmed hat was pale and he was much thinner. He coughed a great deal in between greeting various men. Bentinck followed behind him with a worried look. They greeted each other formally, as the crowds looked on and cheered. Then William announced that Mary was tired and needed to rest for a short time. Mary sent Bentinck back to the ship to greet his eager children, while William and Mary made their way to a nearby small house. Then at last they were alone. They rushed into each other's arms with joyful tears.

'I've missed you so much,' Mary said. 'I was so worried and here you are looking so ill.'

'I'm well enough. You know the English climate doesn't agree with me,' he shrugged. 'I've missed my homeland almost every minute I have been here.' He finished abruptly with a bout of coughing.

Mary ran her hand over his pale forehead. 'How I wish we could just sail home again.'

They both sighed and then William gestured for them to sit down on a wooden bench in the small sitting room. 'We must prepare ourselves,' he said. 'Much is expected of us. We leave for London shortly, where your people await your arrival. I know you don't like this, but you must wear a cheerful face so that all your people will know you are glad to be their queen.'

'How can I be glad?' Mary replied sadly. 'With my father forced to flee his kingdom. I feel so torn between honouring my father and serving the English people.'

William took her hand. 'I did everything I could to ensure your father's safety.'

He shook his head. 'The foolish man got caught trying to escape, so I had to let him escape all over again. He is safe in France now. You had to make a choice between your father and God. Your people deserve the right to worship God without persecution and we can now provide that.' William reached over and raised Mary's face with a gentle hand on each side of her head. 'For the sake of your people you must smile and look glad, regardless of what you feel in your heart. You can do this, I know.'

Mary smiled a little. 'With God's help, I suppose I can. But I'd still rather be in Holland.'

Soon they left the house and began the journey to London. There, William met with some men from the Privy Council and Mary inspected the rooms in the Palace of Whitehall. As she did so she was conscious of people watching her, so she smiled and laughed and admired the furnishings and décor. She found it difficult to ignore her many childhood memories of those rooms while speaking with her courtiers.

The next morning, Mary rose early and walked through the rooms alone, thinking of her father and stepmother. She'd had many happy times with Mary Beatrice when they were younger, and she had treasured her letters. They had grieved together over their lost children. 'How can I do this?' she asked God. Is it right for me to be here? Then she remembered her father's persecution of Protestants. He'd been determined to convert England to Catholicism. He had disbanded Parliament, imprisoned bishops and all who spoke out against him. And he had made his own laws, ignoring the English judicial system. He had broken both God's and man's laws. She knew what she had to do. 'O help me, Heavenly Father. I don't want to be queen, but I will if you require it.'

Later that day, William led Mary into the Banqueting Hall where all the Members of Parliament and the nobility had gathered. As they walked the length of the room, everyone bowed and curtsied. At the far end, a dais had been erected with two armchairs on it with the Canopy of State over top. They took their seats.

The Marquis of Halifax stood to one side and read out the Declaration of Rights, a document that had been drawn up by the Members of Parliament. The marquis read out all the ways that King James had injured England and its people and then invited both William and Mary to be their new king and queen. Both had to agree to rule with Parliament and respect the rights of their subjects. William rose and spoke for both of them, saying they would do their best, with God's help, to rule the kingdom well. He promised they would respect the laws and work with both Houses of Parliament.

Great cheers from within and without the palace rose from the crowds. Freedom had come to England.

Later, Mary lay on her bed, tired out from all the formal duties that followed. She closed her eyes, but sleep wouldn't come. More visions of her past kept flitting across her mind. As she lay still she was gradually aware that women were speaking in the next room. The door was open, so Mary could hear some of what they said.

'Did you see her?' Sarah Churchill's voice asked with contempt. Mary remembered Sarah from her days living in St James's Palace, when Sarah was Mary Beatrice's lady in waiting. Sarah had since become Princess Anne's closest friend, while her husband had served King James.

Someone made a disapproving noise. 'Such foolish behaviour, going from room to room like a housewife. And laughing ...'

'And her father just newly deposed from his throne.' Sarah agreed. 'You'd think she would have more feeling for her father and stepmother who were so good to her. Instead, she couldn't be happier to have them gone. A very hard-hearted queen she will make.'

Mary felt as if she had been stabbed with a knife. How could people think such a thing of her? She was just doing as William had told her to do, appearing cheerful and ready for the task. Was this what it was going to be like to be queen? Always being mistakenly judged and found wanting? She fought away the tears as she rose from the bed. She had to face yet another gathering and hide how she really felt.

The Reluctant Queen

(1689-91)

Two months later, on 11th April, the crowds began to gather outside Westminster Abbey for the coronation. Both William and Mary dreaded the event: William, because he still disliked public ceremonies and display, and Mary because it was the final seal on the position she never wanted. But they put aside their personal feelings to serve the country.

The day started early, with Mary rising at 5 a.m. to attend morning prayer before beginning to dress in the elaborate jewel encrusted gown of gold cloth. Just as her maid had finished dressing her hair, one of her ladies handed her a letter that had been delivered by courier. Recognising her father's handwriting, Mary abruptly ordered everyone to leave.

Her bedchamber quickly cleared of servants and her ladies-in-waiting. With trembling hands she opened it and read the short note.

Daughter,
Until now I have been willing to overlook what
you have done, and thought your obedience to your
husband and compliance to the nations might have
prevailed. But your being crowned is in your own

> *power; if you do it while I and the Prince of Wales*
> *are still living, the curses of an angry father will*
> *fall on you as well as those of a God who commands*
> *obedience to parents.*
>
> *James, King of England*

With tears running down her face, she rose and would have run to William's dressing room, but for the heavy gown. Instead she managed a stately stride, waving aside her ladies as they followed her anxiously down the corridor.

William, dressed in matching coat and breeches of gold cloth, greeted her with a grim face. He had just received news that James had landed in the south of Ireland with an enormous army, planning to conquer the island and then England. After reading Mary's letter, he passed it to Bentinck and several other members of the Privy Council who were standing about the room. As they muttered oaths and shook their heads, William turned to Mary.

Taking her hands in his, he said gently, 'We must not let your father undermine our resolve to do what is right. He had his chance to rule this country and lost it because of his dictatorial reign. We didn't take his throne; he gave it up and fled. Your people invited us here and here we will stay. You must be strong today and show your people how a good queen faces adversity.'

Mary nodded and smiled weakly. 'I'll try.'

William squeezed her hands and then released them. 'Onward, Gentlemen,' he said to his councillors. Then he offered his arm to Mary. 'Your Majesty, your people await you.'

Mary found the coronation service long and the crown heavy on her head. She and William took their oaths to uphold the laws of the land and to defend the truth faith with strong voices. And then they sat on their thrones to accept to the oaths of fealty from each of the nobility and members of parliament. Afterwards, there were celebrations in the streets for the townsfolk and a banquet for the nobility in the Palace of Westminster.

At the end of the day, Mary fell into bed exhausted, but not sleepy. She lay, staring up at the patterned tester, wishing William was here beside her instead of meeting with his Privy Council. She felt lonelier than she had in her life. Gone were the comfortable days in Holland with her small court and relaxed etiquette. Gone were her close friends, replaced now by people who treated her only with distant respect. 'Help me, O God,' she prayed, not for the first time that day. Then she remembered Bishop Compton's text for the coronation sermon.

'When one rules justly over men, ruling in the fear of God, he dawns on them like the morning light, like the sun shining forth on a cloudless morning, like rain that makes grass to sprout from the earth.'[10]

---

[10] 2 Samuel 23:3b-4

'Please help us to rule in your fear,' she prayed as her eyes began at last to close.

The rest of 1689 passed by more quietly than Mary had hoped. William, knowing her distaste for politics, took on all the duties of the monarch, which left her free to find them a new place to live. William's health continued to deteriorate. Living in London with periodic thick fogs, smoky air, and lower standards of housekeeping all contributed to making his breathing more difficult. He coughed incessantly and was losing weight. So Mary purchased Kensington Palace, which stood on higher ground outside the city. She hired architects and builders to renovate the buildings and make sure there was good drainage. She also planned and supervised the garden designs. She enjoyed preparing a new home for William that she hoped would be a refuge from the strains of government as well as a place of recovery. However, she still had to return frequently to Whitehall in London to deal with her own set of governing issues.

Many of the court were turning hostile to William already. Mary, who understood most of the unspoken rules of the English court, sighed heavily when a string of offended courtiers began showing up in her audience room. Many of them complained that her husband was uncivil or he didn't observe the etiquette of the court. Why had he given all the best jobs to his Dutch friends instead of to them? Didn't he realise he owed his throne to them? Why did he insist on keeping his Dutch guards around him? Didn't he trust the English army? And on and on it went.

Mary did her best to soothe their ruffled feelings. She urged them to be more forgiving of William, who after all was new to England. The Dutch did things differently and the English must be patient with him. Even as she said these things, she knew that William would not change. After twelve years of marriage, Mary knew her husband well. He had no time for giving honours and titles to people who hadn't earned them, or playing polite games of 'you help me and I'll help you.' He refused to understand that the English court had a long tradition of giving and receiving favours. After these sessions of serving tea and sympathy, Mary was only too glad to escape back to planning her new house.

But all this changed in the beginning of 1690. William announced he was preparing to leave with the army to meet James in Ireland. Mary's father had spent the previous year marching his army northward, his unruly soldiers looting and pillaging as they went. In anguish the Irish had called for assistance from England.

'You can't go!' Mary complained as she paced about William's study.

William looked up from his desk. 'I must,' he replied flatly. 'Please, let's not have hysterics now. And stop pacing!' He returned to signing documents and rolling the blotter over his signature.

Mary sat down, angrily pushing aside the ribbons hanging from her head dress. Her overskirt, pulled back and held in place by loops of ribbons, had her teetering on the edge of the chair, and her stiff-boned bodice kept her sternly upright.

William, finished with his task, looked up again and surveyed her with disapproval. 'Why can't you act like a queen instead of a silly woman? You took oaths to serve your country and now you must do so. I have organised everything for you.' He waved his hand at the papers on the desk. 'Your Privy Councillors are chosen, all men of good sense who will give you good advice. Just do as they say and you won't go wrong.'

Mary sighed, her anger dissipating at the reminder of her duty. 'But why can't you just send the army? Why do you have to go yourself?'

'It's my duty. How can I be a respected king if I can't lead my own army?'

Mary made a face. 'You want to go,' she accused.

William shrugged. 'Of course, I do. I've missed my army days and I need to get away from the city. You know how much better my health is in the countryside.'

Mary nodded reluctantly. 'Tell me about these new councillors and what issues are most important.'

* * *

Mary watched from the window of her apartments in Whitehall, as William led the combined English and Dutch army through the streets and out of

London. Once more she found herself praying for his safety, knowing the uncertainty of battle. And it was made worse by the fact that he was going to fight her father. How should she pray? Surely not for her father's death? It was so difficult to sort it all out. To distract her from worry, Mary turned to trying to understand her role in governing the country without William.

At first, when she attended a Privy Council meeting, the men seemed surprised to see her. They had thought she would leave all the decisions to them. And at first she did. She listened to the discussion of the issues and to their plans of action without comment. But the more she listened, the less she was impressed with these men. Some were honest but weak, some were lazy and at least two of them were too ambitious to be trusted. She was also distressed to discover that they would often meet informally without her and neglected to tell her what was decided.

But then a crisis occurred that suddenly had them all working together.

On 22nd June, a letter arrived to say the French fleet had been sighted of the coast of Devon. The Council met at once and decided that the English navy must move to repel the French, before they could land. Mary wrote the orders and a courier rushed to deliver them. However, the commander, Lord Torrington, failed to move as quickly as he should have. His fleet was in poor condition: ships unrepaired and sailors unpaid and surly. So he hung back, waiting for some of the Dutch navy to join in and help.

The Council met daily or more often, sending and receiving the latest news. Anger at Lord Torrington's carelessness and lack of courage began to grow; especially after he let the Dutch engage the French fleet while he withdrew to a safe distance. Now in a fury, the Council urged Mary to give orders to have the commander arrested and a new leader chosen. Mary agreed, but hesitated about who to appoint. Meanwhile, the city of London was in turmoil, certain the French ships would break through and sail up the Thames to destroy the city.

Mary surprised herself and her councillors with her cool head. Despite the panic she felt inside and her desperate letters to William reporting on events and asking his advice, she found she was able to listen carefully and formulate plans. God answered her daily prayers for wisdom.

The Dutch States-General were angry with Lord Torrington for sacrificing their ships to protect his own, and the English people called for the naval commander's imprisonment. Mary agreed. She sent Lord Nottingham to the Netherlands to assure the Dutch people she would punish her cowardly commander and then had Torrington arrested and put in the Tower of London. She appointed Lord Russell as the new commander, who set to driving the French away from the coast. Meanwhile, news of William's victory over James' army encouraged everyone and the French navy then withdrew.

Mary was so relieved to receive William's letter, telling her of the Irish campaign. He assured her that her father had escaped any injury and was probably on his way to France, leaving his defeated army behind. It was the best she could have expected from the whole affair.

Once the crisis had passed, Mary turned her attention to some smaller matters that she considered very necessary for her people. Since she had returned to England she had been distressed to see how few people attended church on the Sabbath or kept the day in anyway different from the other six days. Her first thought was to teach people what they might not know, so she issued a proclamation to have sermons that had been preached by various bishops, printed and distributed. She hoped that people would read them and better learn how God wanted them to behave. But when that seemed to have little impact, she decided some new laws were called for. So, with the agreement of her Council, she issued more proclamations, closing businesses on Sundays and outlawing public drunkenness. She knew some people snickered at her for being too pious, but she ignored them. Mary was convinced that her duty as queen also included instructing her people on the right way to live.

* * *

When William returned in September he praised Mary for her handling of the crisis and her work with her Council. Mary was pleased, but not enough to want to continue on with governing. She gladly handed all the duties back to William and retired to Kensington Palace to supervise the last of the building and decorating.

If only it had been possible to leave England in William's hands permanently, she would have been perfectly happy. But it was not to be.

Sisters

(1689-1692)

Mary had always loved her sister, although they were very different from each other. Even as children, when given the choice, they usually chose different activities. Anne preferred to sit quietly with one or two friends, while Mary enjoyed dancing and other social events. Now that they were both older and married, they discovered at least two similarities between them. They both loved their husbands dearly and they both longed for children. Mary had learned early in her married life that she wouldn't have any children. Anne had been pregnant every year since she married, but all her children had died. So both sisters were overjoyed when Anne gave birth to a baby boy in July of 1689, who was determined to live. Anne and her husband, George, named the baby, William, in honour of the king. The baby was also given the title of Duke of Gloucester and everyone then called him Gloucester.

Mary was so pleased to be asked to be Gloucester's godparent and she took her duties very seriously. She visited her little nephew often, enjoyed discussing his development with her sister and even invited him to be presented when they had visiting dignitaries. Anne, of course, was very pleased with her sister's love for her son, but she also saw an opportunity to ask for some favours.

'I don't think I'm asking for too much,' Anne said, adjusting her bulky frame more comfortably on the settee in her receiving room. She sipped her hot chocolate and eyed her sister over the china cup. 'Gloucester may be just a small infant, but he does come with his own household of servants. We will need the extra space to house them all.'

Mary too was sipping her chocolate and playing for time to form the right words to refuse Anne. 'I understand your need,' Mary replied kindly. 'But you know all the apartments in Whitehall are spoken for. The ones you want are already promised to Portsmouth and I can hardly take them away.'

Anne replaced her cup with a force that shook the saucer. 'Well, I'd hardly be happy with the leavings of Portsmouth anyway!' she replied. 'If he's more acceptable to you than your own sister, then so be it. Now I think I need to lie down. I'm still not feeling myself after the birth.' Anne signalled to one of her ladies to come and help her up.

Mary rose too and went over to Anne. 'I'm sorry, Anne. You know I'd change it if I could but then there'd be more complaints from others about who gets what favour. It's really not that easy.'

Anne turned away and over her shoulder Mary saw Sarah Churchill, now Duchess of Marlborough, watching and listening with a sour expression. Sarah had become Anne's closest friend over the years, but Mary still didn't like her.

Sarah turned her gaze to Anne and spoke, 'Possibly the queen could spare you Cockpit House nearby for your household?' Sarah looked back at Mary with raised eyebrows.

Mary refused to reply directly to Sarah. Instead she turned her back on the woman and said to Anne, 'If Cockpit House would suit you, you may certainly have it. Now I'll let you rest. Kiss little Gloucester for me.'

The sisters parted with Anne annoyed and Mary bothered by the disagreement. But there was worse to come. Not long afterwards, William and Mary learned that Anne had sent a request to Parliament concerning her allowance. She asked for two things: to have it controlled by Parliament and to raise the amount significantly, using her son as the reason for more money. William and Mary were both hurt and angry.

'How could she do that?' Mary asked as she sat at dinner with William. 'She knows that her allowance, like any other heir to the throne, is taken care of by the king. That's what happened when my father ruled.'

William gave an impolite snort. 'Not that he actually sent you your allowance as his heir. Somehow he never got around to it.'

'Well, if that's what Anne is worried about, she shouldn't. Of course you will see that she gets her allowance. But by asking Parliament to do it, she's telling the whole country she doesn't trust us,' Mary complained.

William took some fish offered by the attending servant before replying. 'I think I know who's behind this: Marlborough's wife. I don't trust those two. They both served your father and his wife before conveniently changing sides when the people invited us to take the throne. I suspect the only real loyalty they have is to themselves and they're using your sister to stir up distrust against us. However, we can't fight with your sister in public. I'll send Lord Shrewsbury to speak to her and see if we can't work something out quietly.'

Mary agreed, although she'd have much rather found a way to get rid of Sarah, the Duchess of Marlborough, from her sister's household. However, the whole incident didn't turn out well. Mary knew how stubborn her sister could be over matters she thought were important, so not even the reasonable suggestions put forward by Lord Shrewsbury could convince Anne that she should change her mind. In the end, Parliament did take over the administration of Anne's allowance and there were enough members of Parliament sympathetic to her to vote her a large increase. Mary was not happy, but with William's encouragement she decided to let the matter go.

The following year, when William was away in Ireland fighting against her father, Mary continued to visit with Anne and little Gloucester, and for the most part they remained friendly. Prince George went with William to fight in the campaign, which made Anne very proud. But when the men returned, Anne was displeased to learn that George had been given very little to do. William had not invited him to any strategy sessions or let him lead any part of the army. Anne was sure William meant it as an insult. And then to make matters worse, when William left for Holland in January of 1691 to defend the Netherlands from the French, he refused to take George with him. Anne was furious. So when it was time to celebrate Anne's birthday on 6th February, Mary arrived at Cockpit House with worry in the pit of her stomach. She didn't want to slight her sister by ignoring her birthday, but she also didn't want to listen to her complain about William with Sarah smirking in the background.

'Welcome, Your Majesty,' Prince George said, bowing as best he could with his rounded middle. He was as tall as Mary and quite portly, with a smiling face and a curly white wig. 'See, my dear, here is your sister, the queen, come to join us at dinner.'

Mary smiled at her brother-in-law, relieved to see him cheerful. Maybe he didn't really want to go with William to the continent after all. Maybe it had been more Anne's idea. Mary then went over to her sister, who was struggling to get up from the settee. 'No, no, sister, please don't get up. You must not exert yourself while expecting a baby,' and Mary kissed Anne on the cheek.

Anne smiled. 'Thank you. And thank you for coming. I thought you might find the affairs of state too much to spare the time.'

Mary laughed. 'Short of a war, nothing would keep me from seeing you. It's such a relief to be away from all that even for just a few hours. So tell me, how are you feeling? When is the baby due? And how is my darling Gloucester?'

The evening passed quickly with lots of talk and laughter, as if nothing had happened between them. Mary was so relieved she even stayed longer than she had planned and promised to visit again soon.

Feeling so encouraged, Mary began to take on more social engagements, doing her best to encourage her people that she really did care about their everyday lives. She visited retired soldiers at Chelsea Hospital, hoping to cheer up those who were too old or badly injured to care for themselves. And she began accepting invitations to dine at the homes of various Members of Parliament. Her Privy Councillors were more receptive to her comments and suggestions and, overall, Mary thought her time on the throne that year had gone well. Nevertheless, she was very glad to see William when he arrived home in April, and very disappointed when he left again in May and stayed away until October.

When William finally returned, he swept into Whitehall late at night, waking up the whole palace.

He strode into Mary's bedchamber and informed her she was to get dressed because he wanted to take her to their home at Kensington Palace. Mary threw herself joyfully into his arms and then promised to get ready as quickly as possible. Riding in the carriage, wrapped in furs and snuggled up close to William, Mary felt both wonderful relief and giddy delight that William was back and she could relax. However, it was short-lived. William remained, but life around them suddenly became a tangled mess.

It began one night in November, when a servant rushed into their bedchamber at Kensington Palace shouting, 'Fire! Fire!' Everyone escaped quickly into the garden, with servants scrambling to carry out the treasured paintings, china and jewels onto the lawn. Mary's ladies wailed as if they were dying. Fortunately, the fire was put out quickly and everyone was able to move back in the next morning. While repairs were made, the servants spent their time returning all the treasures to their proper places. Mary was thankful no one had been injured.

Not long afterwards, a fire of a different sort began. From the beginning of William's reign a group of people opposed William being king. They were still loyal to King James and called themselves Jacobites, a form of the name James. They believed William had stolen the throne from James. Some of them stayed in contact with James and encouraged him to invade England and re-take the throne. But it was all done as secretly as possible, so it was difficult to prove who was a Jacobite and who was not.

Rumours began circulating that Sarah's husband, the Duke of Marlborough, was a Jacobite. William ignored the rumours and told Mary he could do nothing until there was proof that Marlborough had committed treason. Then Marlborough, acting on advice from James himself, gave a speech in the House of Lords at the end of the year, suggesting that all foreign-born men be removed from their government jobs and their positions given to Englishmen. He never actually named William, who, of course, was Dutch, but everyone knew who he meant.

At last, William had something to prove the Duke of Marlborough's disloyalty. Immediately after the Christmas season, William dismissed him from his position in the palace and told him to leave without any public announcement. But it quickly became public knowledge and people took sides in the matter. Feelings ran very high. Some felt that Marlborough, who was very popular with the people, should be allowed to speak his mind, and some even agreed with him. Some just thought there were too many Dutchmen about and, while they would keep William, they wanted most of his men sent home. Then there was the group who supported William and Mary and thought all Jacobites should be thrown in prison for treason. No one was happy, especially not Mary or Anne.

Mary was glad to see Marlborough leave the court, but was amazed to discover that his wife, Sarah, still remained in Anne's household. Mary sent a short letter to her sister, telling her that Sarah should be dismissed from her service because of her husband's disloyalty. Anne, angry at the entire matter, took her feelings out on Mary.

'I will not dismiss my closest friend. I can't imagine life without her at my side, helping and encouraging me,' she wrote. She went on to say if Mary insisted then Anne would remove her household, including Gloucester, from the court and out of Mary's sight. Then, without any further notice, Anne did just that. She moved her family and servants to Syon House, ten miles outside of London.

Mary was heartbroken, but also very angry. How dare her sister defy her so publicly, causing the entire court to take sides! Did Anne regret the part she had played in her father's downfall? Did she agree with the Duke of Marlborough that all foreigners should be sent home, including William himself? Had her own sister betrayed her and joined the Jacobites?

Mary tried once more to sort things out with her sister, two months later, when she heard that Anne had given birth to a baby girl who died within an hour. Mary went immediately to Syon House to comfort her sister and to discuss the matter of Sarah once more.

Sarah greeted Mary at the door of Anne's bedchamber, curtsying but not in the least ashamed to be seen in the queen's presence. Mary almost said something to Sarah, but chose instead to see her sister. Anne was propped up in her tester bed, her eyes red and her face very pale. Mary went to give her sister a kiss, but Anne turned her face away.

'Oh, Anne! Can we not agree?' Mary asked. When Anne didn't answer, Mary changed the topic. 'I'm so sorry about your daughter. I know your sorrow and I will pray that you will know God's comfort.'

Then there was silence as Anne continued to study the wall beside the bed. Mary sighed. 'Will you not speak to me?'

'Not until you accept Sarah as my friend,' Anne replied.

'No, you know I cannot and remain loyal to my husband, the king. I'm sorry for you, Anne, about your baby, but Sarah must be dismissed. Until then, we have nothing more to say to each other.'

Mary left Syon House with a sore and angry heart.

Finding Peace
(1692-1694)

A black cloud hung over Mary for the rest of 1692. Things just seemed to go from bad to worse. William had left for Holland as usual in the spring, leaving Mary to rule England. She and her Privy Councillors were used to one another now and worked reasonably well together. But life was still full of anxiety.

On 1st May, an informer came forward with proof that the Duke of Marlborough had committed treason, so Mary had him arrested and sent to the Tower of London. At the same time, an assassination plot against her had been uncovered. With fear and trembling she insisted that she would carry on her usual routine, reviewing the troops and visiting the navy ports before the navy sailed out to meet the French yet again. She prayed all the while she appeared in public, asking God to protect her and to help her appear cheerful to her people.

The officers were very impressed with her courage when they heard about the foiled assassination plot. 'Thank you so much, Your Majesty for coming out to rally the men. They are in sore need of encouragement,' one captain said as he welcomed her aboard his ship.

Mary nodded sadly. 'Yes, the unsettledness of the court and the country in the last year is being felt everywhere, and it doesn't help that the French are lurking off our coast again. But I would like to help the men, and I think some extra pay will encourage them all,' she finished with smile.

The captain grinned. 'Indeed, ma'am, it would. Would you like to tell them?'

Mary nodded and turned to the sailors assembled on the deck in straight lines. She then delivered the short speech she had given many times on the ships and on land. She told them of her pride in them as English sailors ready to do battle to protect their homeland. That made them all stand a little straighter. Then she informed them of the extra pay that would be waiting for them when they returned, and of her plans to build a hospital at Greenwich to care for disabled seamen. The sailors gave the queen their grateful cheers. And two weeks later, the navy won a decisive victory over the French.

Mary's black mood didn't lift, even after the victory. The summer months brought more problems. In June, the informant, who had accused the Duke of Marlborough of treason, confessed he had lied, so Mary was forced to release the duke and arrest the informer. It rankled that Sarah was telling everyone how foolish Mary had been to have believed the charges in the first place. Mary ignored her, especially when more serious news arrived at the palace.

The French navy, still smarting from their defeat, decided to take their revenge on some Dutch and English merchant ships, completely destroying the poorly armed ships and their cargo. Over £1 million was lost, a huge blow to the English economy. Many merchants lost all their money and had no goods to sell to recover it. Then, to make matters worse, a new assassination plot was uncovered; this time against William, timed for when he returned to England. Worst of all, the plot was traced back to Mary's father, James.

Mary dismissed her ladies and servants and fled to her chapel to pray. Falling to her knees at the communion rail, she poured out her grief to God. She started with all the problems of state: the continual threats of attack by the French navy, the internal threat of the Jacobite faction, the assassination plots, and even the in-fighting of her councillors and Members of Parliament. Everyone seemed to be in turmoil. Then she started on her personal list of grievances: William's continual absences, necessary she knew, but she missed him terribly, her quarrel with her sister that appeared to have no end, and the terrible ache inside her for the children God had withheld from her.

'Why does it have to be this way? Why have you made it so difficult? How can I possibly do this on my own?' she prayed, lost in a sea of tears and self-pity.

After a time, the answer came quietly into her mind. 'My grace is sufficient for you, for my power is made perfect in weakness.'[11]

After much time, Mary rose stiffly. She had cried out all the tears she had in her and felt exhausted. Yet there

[11] 2 Corinthians 12:9

was some hope in her heart too. God was with her and she knew his strength and power would see her through. Opening the door to the chapel, she found Dr Burnett in the corridor surrounded by a group of worried ladies and some Privy Councillors. They all turned to her with concerned faces.

'Are you all right, Your Majesty?' Dr Burnet asked.

Mary smiled weakly. 'I'm fine. I just needed to consult with the King of Kings before tending to my own duties.'

* * *

When William returned at the end of October, he was in poor health and a bad mood. He criticised much of what Mary had done that year and she fled back to Kensington to nurse her wounded feelings. Let him sort it all out then, she thought irritably. And good luck to him, she added, not meaning it at all.

Mary spent much of that winter alone by choice. She'd had enough of politics and people complaining. She shut herself up with her ladies, spending a good deal of time reading her Bible and devotional works and praying. When she was not at her devotions she tended to some of the charitable works she had set up: the schools and hospitals in Ireland and the naval hospital in Greenwich. She was also pleased to be approached by the Reverend James Blair to found a college in the colony of Virginia. Mr Blair named it after William and Mary. William himself approved the charter and gave the college a substantial amount of money. But Mary played a slightly different role. Mr Blair had told her of the need to train more young men to be missionaries to reach out to the Indian tribes around them. Mary donated £600 of her own money to help.

William followed his usual pattern over the next two years, leaving in the spring and returning in the fall. Mary wearily took up her usual duties and gladly set them down again when he returned. By 1694, the strain was beginning to show on both of them and by the November neither one of them was very well.

William was confined to his bed shortly after his 44th birthday, while Mary fussed over him trying to get him to take the rest he needed. By the time he had regained his strength, Mary herself fell ill.

Mary spent the first part of December resting quietly in her bedchamber, but then felt well enough to join William at dinner. It was there he broke the news to her that he wouldn't be staying for Christmas. Instead, he was planning to return to the Netherlands earlier than usual to sort out some governmental tangles and try to get his army ready early for the usual spring assaults of the French.

Mary pushed away the plate of food in front of her. She didn't cry or even lose her temper with him. She felt too tired to argue or plead. 'I wish you wouldn't go,' was all she could muster. 'I need you.'

William began his usual reply to this conversation they had every year, but stopped and looked at her more closely. 'You shouldn't have gotten up. You still look unwell. Let me help you to your bedchamber.'

Mary didn't argue. She let William take her arm and guide her down the corridor where they were met by her concerned ladies. William handed her over to them with instructions to put her to bed.

'You won't leave without saying goodbye, will you?' Mary asked.

William kissed her on the forehead. 'Of course not. Now sleep well.'

Mary didn't sleep well, even after one of her ladies brought her some hot chocolate. As she lay awake, she began to think about dying. If she should die, there were certain things she wanted to do. So she rose quietly so no one would hear her and rush in. She went to her desk where she kept her letters and diaries. Leafing through them, she pulled out papers here and there and threw them into the fireplace, where they burned up quickly. Then she sat down to write.

Wrapped in several shawls over her nightgown, Mary wrote a long letter to William and then some shorter ones to friends and last of all a Will with instructions for a simple funeral.

Mary couldn't have said why she was doing this, if anyone should happen to ask. It was just a conviction that it should be done. Once she finished she tidied her desk and headed back to bed. Then she had a thought. She went over to her jewel cases sitting on her dressing table and fished through the various beautiful pieces for a ruby ring. It was the first ring William had ever given her. She remembered how ungracious she had been when he presented it when they were first engaged, but how she treasured it now. Putting it on her finger, she climbed back into bed and fell asleep.

Mary's premonition sadly came true. She knew within a few days, when the rash first appeared. Smallpox was raging through the city of London, a disease Mary had escaped, until now. Already weak from illness, she quickly became worse with a high fever and then developed additional symptoms of St Anthony's Fire.

In a panic, William cancelled his plans to leave and called in the doctors. They tried a number of painful cures, but nothing stopped the progress of the disease. William had a camp bed moved into Mary's bedchamber. He refused to eat and slept only when Mary slept, spending the rest of his time by her bed, keeping her head cool with cold cloths and pleading with her to get well.

By Christmas Day, everyone knew it was certain that she would die. Mary's ladies were amazed and frightened when William burst into tears at the news. But it was Mary who comforted him. 'You mustn't grieve. You know that where I go there will be no more suffering. I would ask you to pray for me, especially right near the end when I can no longer pray for myself.'

William, with tears in his eyes and voice, did as she asked and prayed with her and for her.

Mary lingered for three more days before finally closing her eyes for the last time.

Epilogue

Mary was thirty two when she died. She had reigned as queen for only five years. William was almost inconsolable. He collapsed and was gravely ill for almost a month. All of England was stunned at the sudden death of their queen and the depth of William's love for her. Since William rarely showed his emotions in public, most people assumed that their marriage had been one of convenience and not love. Now everyone began to fear that William would die too. But by the end of January 1695, he recovered enough to meet with Princess Anne.

Anne met William in a private room at Whitehall where Anne made her apologies for her past behaviour and William accepted them. He then publicly announced that Anne was the next heir to the throne. He never wanted to marry again, so her place in the line of succession was secure. This announcement gained William a great deal of approval among the people.

Because of William's slow recovery, Mary's funeral was postponed until 5th March so that William could attend. It was an elaborate affair because her last Will wasn't found until later. People lined the streets and wept as her coffin passed by, and Westminster Abbey was full. In his sermon, the Archbishop of Canterbury took time to list Mary's virtues of knowledge of the Scriptures, wisdom in governing, piety toward God and charity toward others. All of these were the fruits of God's grace in her life. He urged everyone to not just mourn her loss, but to look to God for help to live as Mary did, in pleasing obedience to God.

The Archbishop concluded with the verse in Acts 13:36 to sum up Mary's life. He compared Mary to King David of the Old Testament.

> For David, after he had served the purpose of God in his own generation, fell asleep.

Mary served God's purpose for the time she lived. He used her to assist those in need, especially the persecuted Huguenots, who suffered terribly in France before escaping to European Protestant countries. In both the Netherlands and England, Mary provided for their physical needs and encouraged them in their Christian lives. God also used Mary as an example of how a Christian should live, even in difficult circumstances. For most of her life she was at the mercy of the kings in her family: her uncle Charles II, her father, James II and her husband, William III. Even though she had few choices in her life, she still committed her way to the King of Kings, who was her greatest source of strength.

With Gratitude

When we are young, our parents always tell us to say 'thank you' for everything, from gifts we receive to someone holding a door for us. It's all part of being polite and showing a grateful spirit. And it is something we learn so that we will continue to be thankful throughout our lives. Well, here is where I will say my 'thank yous'.

It takes more than one person to write a book, even though only one name usually appears on the cover. The author does work very hard to write the book, but it can't be done without help. First, I would like to thank my publisher, Christian Focus, and my editor, Catherine Mackenzie for their willingness to publish my books and for Catherine's encouragement as I worked through this project. My thanks should also go to Irene Roberts, Catherine's editorial assistant, who has a keen eye for detail and all those little mistakes I make that need correcting.

The second group to thank are my writing friends. Donna Farley and I have been friends since childhood and have read each other's stories from our earliest efforts until now. Donna has been very helpful with plot problems and making sure I have tied up all my loose ends. Sharon L. Bratcher is a newer friend, but nonetheless helpful as she carefully reads my work and makes useful, honest comments.

Finally, I must thank my husband, Sandy. He is two helpers rolled into one. As a librarian there isn't much he can't find out for me. I just have to ask and he beavers away until he finds the answers to my questions. As my husband, he is my chief encourager: egging me on when I get discouraged, reading and critiquing all my work, and telling everyone he can, to read my books. As a writer himself, he understands when I get lost in my work and forget such small things as cooking a meal or making sure his clothing has been washed and pressed. He is a very patient man!

Marriage 17th Century Style

Mary was horrified at the announcement of her marriage to her cousin William. But she shouldn't have been surprised. In the 17th century a young woman or man didn't usually choose their own marriage partner. Parents or guardians did the choosing, and almost everyone approved of this way of planning a marriage. Parents reasoned that because they loved their children they would choose someone who could love and care for their beloved child. Once the couple were married, they were expected to grow to love each other within the marriage.

Royal marriages also had other considerations. A royal person had lots of wealth and power, so you would think that their lives would have been better. And in many ways that was true. Mary never had to worry about having enough food, clothing or places to live. But a royal person's wealth didn't make every part of their lives easy. They also had responsibilities, and one of those was to marry whoever would help their country. Mary was required to marry her cousin, William, as part of a plan to bring a peaceful end to the war between their two countries. That might seem unfair, but that was how politics often interfered with the lives of royalty, especially women.

After the wedding, Mary's marriage followed the common pattern of most royal marriages. Her marriage was not a private one. She was expected to have her own household of servants and companions (ladies in waiting) in her own set of apartments in the palace. Her husband, William, had the same. This was not to prevent them from spending time together, because they did. They even slept in the same bed, whenever William was 'at home'. They had separate households to allow them to carry out their duties as leaders of their countries. This was their job, just as if they went to work each day the way most adults do in this century. William would have ambassadors meet him in Honselaerskijck Palace as well as military commanders or representatives from the States General. Meanwhile, Mary would receive important visitors from England, ambassadors from other countries and leading Dutch women. She did this in order to work quietly behind the scenes: listening for any complaints or problems that might be brewing among people, finding out who was in need of help or giving the women an opportunity to express their opinions on what was happening in the country. Mary could then pass these things on to William. Later, when she was queen, Mary could address these same issues herself. William and Mary essentially lived 'at the office' and their private lives came second to their responsibilities as monarchs.

Lastly, you might wonder why Mary was married so young. In the 17th century it was very common for a young woman to marry in her middle to late teens, especially those of the upper classes. Because of disease and hygiene issues, the average life expectancy of women was usually around forty years of age, if they survived the dangers of giving birth to children. And since children often died before they reached the age of two, women married early in order to have as many children as possible in the hope that some would survive to adulthood. Those children who did survive were then expected to take on the same responsibilities as their parents, when it came time for them to marry.

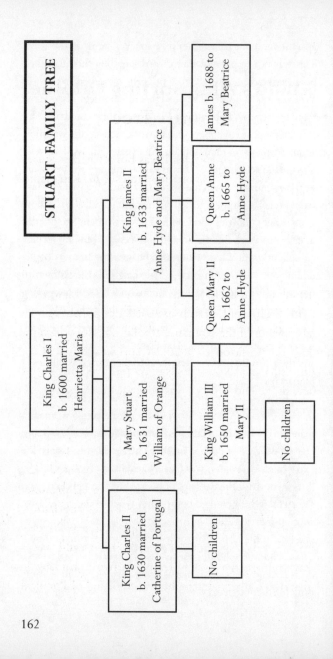

STUART FAMILY TREE

King Charles I b. 1600 married Henrietta Maria

- **King Charles II** b. 1630 married Catherine of Portugal
  - No children
- **Mary Stuart** b. 1631 married William of Orange
  - **King William III** b. 1650 married Mary II
    - No children
- **King James II** b. 1633 married Anne Hyde and Mary Beatrice
  - **Queen Mary II** b. 1662 to Anne Hyde
  - **Queen Anne** b. 1665 to Anne Hyde
  - **James** b. 1688 to Mary Beatrice

Who's Who: Sorting Out the Family Tree

Charles I was born Charles Stuart, son of King James I (of King James Bible fame). He became king in 1625, when his father died and the same year he married Henrietta Maria, daughter of the King of France. He had a difficult time trying to run his kingdom his way instead of working with Parliament, which annoyed the politicians. He also favoured the Roman Catholic religion which put him out of favour with the Church of England and the Puritans. Not surprisingly, civil war broke out and in the end Charles was beheaded and his wife and children fled to France.

Charles II, son of Charles I, became king in 1660 after the civil war was over and the people wanted their king back. This Charles promised to support the Protestant faith as part of his coronation vows even though secretly he would rather have remained a Roman Catholic. Two years later he married Catherine, daughter of the King of Portugal.

Sadly, they had no children. Charles was known as the Merry Monarch because he liked to 'party,' and he was not a faithful husband. As a result he had a number of illegitimate children, none of whom could inherit his throne.

Mary Stuart, sister of Charles II was a year younger than her brother and she was sent to marry William II of Orange in the Netherlands. It was not a happy marriage and Mary was very snooty to her Dutch subjects. She gave birth to one son, William, who eventually became William III of England, Scotland and Ireland. Her husband died eight days before her son was born and she died when her son was ten years old.

James, Duke of York, was Charles II and Mary's younger brother. He never forgave the English people for beheading his father because he believed very strongly in the Divine Right of Kings (meaning that what the king says, goes, because God had made him king). He was also a committed Roman Catholic and not afraid to say so, which made him very unpopular when he became king. Unfortunately, his moral behaviour was as bad as his brother Charles, which meant his wives were unhappy in their marriages. Yes, I said wives, because James married twice. His first wife, Anne Hyde, died of cancer. He then married Mary

Beatrice from Italy, who was a relative of the pope. His religion and autocratic manner led to James' downfall. He became king when his brother died in 1685, but he only reigned three years before he was ousted from his throne by his daughter, Mary, and her husband, William of Orange.

Mary II was born Mary Stuart, having the same name as her Aunt Mary Stuart, who had died in the Netherlands two years before Mary II's birth. And the similarities didn't stop there. Mary II's uncle Charles II set up a marriage between his niece Mary and his nephew William (his sister Mary's son). Confused? Well, the easiest way to understand it is, Mary and William were first cousins as well as husband and wife. This Mary had a much happier marriage and was loved by her Dutch subjects. Mary assumed she would spend the rest of her life in the Netherlands until her father caused so much fuss in England that some of the English nobility asked Mary and William to come over and take the throne from him. And so they did, being crowned William III and Mary II.

William III of England and of Orange was born eight days after his father died, which made him Prince William of Orange and Stadtholder of the Low Countries when he was only minutes old. He never really knew his mother because his grandmother became his guardian and she didn't like her daughter-in-law one bit. William grew up with tutors and fell in love with army life. He had plenty of practice at leading the Dutch army into battle because the French wanted to take over his country. William was short on stature, only five feet 6 inches (1.68 metres), but he had a big heart for his people. He chose Mary as his wife because she had the qualities he was looking for: royal birth, pleasant personality and she loved God. At first the marriage was rocky, but they soon learned to love each other and they were a good team as rulers in both the Netherlands and Britain.

 Anne Stuart was Mary II's only surviving sibling. They were three years apart, but never really close. Anne had bad eyesight, which meant she found her studies difficult and was rather clumsy. She suffered in comparison to her sister in looks and height. Anne married George of Denmark, who by all accounts was a very dull man. But they suited each other well and had a long, happy marriage. Anne gave birth to five living children, but none survived to adulthood. This caused her a great deal of sorrow. Anne became queen after William III died in 1702 and reigned for twelve years.

Glossary

Barge: a roomy flat-bottomed boat used for transporting people or goods on rivers or canals.

Bleeding: a common medical practice in the 17th century. When a patient was ill, the doctor would make small cuts in the patient's arms and fill small bowls with their blood. It was based on the theory that the illness would leave the body through the blood.

Bodice: the upper part of a woman's dress, separate from the skirt.

Breeches: short trousers covering the hips and thighs, usually snug fitting just above or below the knee.

Cassock: an ankle length garment with close fitting sleeves, worn by Anglican clergy.

Catechism: a summary of Christian doctrine in the form of questions and answers.

Chaplain: (in the 17th century) a clergyman appointed to a royal household to conduct worship services in a chapel and offer spiritual instruction to their employer.

Confirmation: a Christian ceremony conducted by a priest or bishop in the Anglican Church that confers full membership on the person being confirmed.

Courier: a messenger.

Courtiers: people of noble birth, part of the king and queen's court.

Cravat: early form of a man's tie, made up of long strips of cloth tied at the neck.

Fealty: swearing or promising loyalty to a king or queen.

Governess: a woman chosen by parents or guardians of a child to oversee the care and education of that child.

Heir Apparent: person next in line to the English throne.

Huguenot: a French Protestant.

Jacobites: a group of English people who were loyal to James II, especially after he was deposed as the king of England.

Kloven: a game played on ice, which is a cross between golf and hockey.

Looting: stealing goods, usually during a war or a riot.

Parliament: the governing body in England made up the House of Lords (nobility appointed by the king or queen) and the House of Commons (elected men).

Peperkoek: gingerbread, also called sweet cake.

Periwig: a highly stylised wig worn as a headdress by men in the 17th century.

Poffertjes: a traditional Dutch batter treat resembling pancakes. They are made from yeast and buckwheat flour and served with powdered sugar and butter.

Pillaging: to steal using violence, especially in wartime.

Privy Council: a group of advisors appointed by the king or queen to give advice on government matters.

St Anthony's Fire: a disease caused by fungus in rye and wheat grain. Over time this poisoning causes painful burning sensations in the arms and legs and painful muscle cramping.

Small Clothing: underclothing or handkerchiefs.

Smallpox: an infectious viral disease that resulted in high fevers and rash. The rash usually developed into large infected pimples that left scars, if the person survived. In the 17th century there was no cure. The disease was common. Death rate was very high.

Stadtholder: from the Dutch word which means, 'steward'. The Dutch didn't have a monarch at this time. Instead they had a leader who was considered the chief magistrate, but did not have the unlimited power of a king or queen.

States-General: the governing body in the Netherlands made up of leading citizens. This group worked with the Stadtholder to rule the Netherlands.

Tenets: the main principles or doctrines that are true in Christianity.

Tester Bed: a four poster bed with a canopy. The canopy was called a tester.

Timber-heeled shoes: fabric shoes with wooden heel and sole.

Waistcoat: a vest worn by men over a shirt and under a jacket.

Warming pan: a wide, flat brass pan on a long handle, filled with hot coals and used for warming a bed.

Bibliography

Barnett, Correlli. *The First Churchill: Marlborough, Soldier and Statesman*. New York: G.P. Putnam's Sons, 1974.

Bathurst, Benjamin. *Letters of Two Queens*. London: Robert Holden & Co. Ltd, 1924.

Bowen, Marjorie. *The Third Mary Stuart: Mary of York, Orange & England*, being a character study with memoirs and letters of Queen Mary II of England, 1662-1694. London: John Lane The Bodley Head Limited, 1929.

Braun & Schneider. *Historic Costume in Pictures: over 1450 costumes on 125 plates*. Toronto: Dover Publications, 1975.

Brooke, Iris. *English Costume of the Seventeenth Century*. 2nd ed. London: Adam and Charles Black, 1950.

Cannon, John and Griffiths, Ralph. *The Oxford Illustrated History of the British Monarchy*. Oxford: Oxford University Press, 1988.

Grun, Bernard. *The Timetables of History: a Horizontal Linkage of People and Events*. 4th ed. New York: Touchstone, 2006.

Hamilton, Elizabeth. *William's Mary: a biography of Mary II*. New York: Taplinger Publishing Co. 1972.

Hansen, Henny Harald. *Costume Cavalcade*: 685 examples of history costume in colour. London: Methuen and Co., 1956.

Hoak, Dale and Mordechai Feingold. *The World of William and Mary: Anglo-Dutch perspectives on the Revolution of 1688-89*. Stanford: Stanford University Press, 1996.

Peacock, John. *Costume 1066-1990's: a complete guide to English costume design and history*. Rev. ed. London: Thames & Hudson, 1994.

Pescio, Claudio. *Rembrandt and Seventeenth Century Holland*. English Language Text. New York: Peter Bedrick Books, 1995.

Picard, Liza. *Restoration London: Everyday life in London 1660-1670*. London: Phoenix, 2003.

Tenison, Thomas. *A Sermon Preached at the Funeral of Her Late Majesty Queen Mary of Ever Blessed Memory, Upon March 5, 1694 by His Grace Thomas, Lord Archbishop of Canterbury*. Dublin: 1695

Van Der Kiste, John. *William and Mary*. Phoenix Mill, Gloucestershire: Sutton Publishing, 2003.

Van Der Zee, Henri and Barbara. *William and Mary*. New York: Alfred A. Knopf, 1973.

Waller, Maureen. *Sovereign Ladies: the Six Reigning Queens of England*. New York: St Martin's Press, 2006.

Waller, Maureen. *Ungrateful Daughters: the Stuart Princesses who stole their father's crown*. New York: St Martin's Press, 2002.

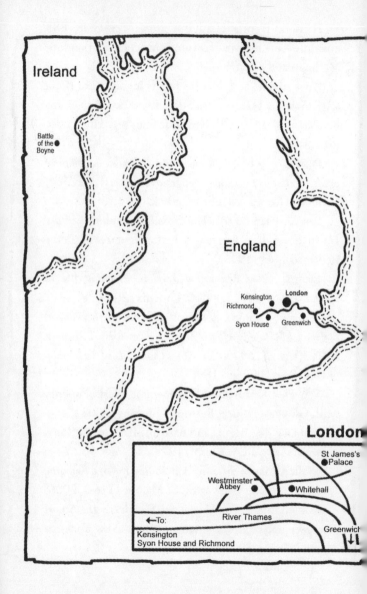

Ireland

Battle
of the ●
Boyne

England

Kensington   ● London
Richmond   ●
       ●   ●
Syon House   Greenwich

London

St James's
● Palace

Westminster ●   ● Whitehall
Abbey

←To: River Thames
Kensington
Syon House and Richmond   Greenwich
                                              ↓↑

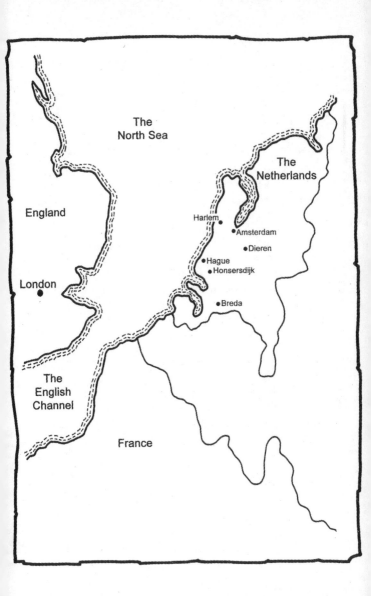

The North Sea

The Netherlands

England

Harlem

Amsterdam

Dieren

Hague
Honsersdijk

London

Breda

The English Channel

France

Timeline

1662	Mary Stuart born on 30th April.
1665	Great Plague of London.
1667	First human blood transfusion was administered by Dr Jean-Baptiste Dennys.
1668	Isaac Newton built the first reflecting telescope.
1671	Mary's mother died. Mary and her sister Anne moved to Richmond Palace.
1673	Mary Beatrice married James, Duke of York and became Mary's stepmother.
1676	Ole Rømer made the first quantitative measurements of the speed of light.
1676	Mary moved back to London to be her stepmother's companion. Mary's confirmation and first communion.
1677	Ice cream became popular in Paris.
1677	Mary married her cousin William on 4th November.
1677	William and Mary moved to Holland.
1678	John Bunyan's *Pilgrim's Progress* was published.
1678	William and Mary expected a baby. William went to war.
1683	Mary started her involvement in charity work.
1683	River Thames froze over.
1684	Mary helped Huguenot refugees from France.
1685	King Charles 1, Mary's uncle died. Mary's father became King James II.
1685	First organised street lighting introduced to London.

1687	King James II of England challenged Mary to read about Roman Catholicism, wanting her to convert to it.
1688	William and his army went to seek to remove King James II from the throne.
1688	Anne Bentinck, Mary's companion, died.
1689	Mary and Anne Bentinck's children returned to England.
	Mary and William became Queen and King of England, Scotland and Ireland.
1689	Coronation ceremony on 11th April.
1690	Clarinet invented in Nuremberg.
1690	William and his army went to Ireland to fight Mary's father James.
	Mary left to rule on her own.
1691	Mary and her sister, Anne, had disagreement about Sarah, Anne's lady-in-waiting.
	Sarah's husband was not loyal to King William.
1692	Sarah's husband, the Duke of Marlborough, was accused of treason and sent to the Tower of London.
1692	Earthquake and tsunami in Jamaica killed over 2000 people.
1692	Duke of Marlborough released from the Tower of London as the informer said he had lied.
1693	Mary and William continued to rule England, Scotland and Ireland and Holland.
	Mary is burdened by all the difficulties.
1694	Mary caught smallpox.
1694	Mary died on 28th December.
1695	Funeral at Westminster Abbey on 5th March.

CHRISTIAN FOCUS PUBLICATIONS

Christian   Christian   CF4K   Mentor
Focus   Heritage

Christian Focus Publications publishes books for adults and children under its four main imprints: Christian Focus, Christian Heritage, CF4K and Mentor. Our books reflect that God's Word is reliable and Jesus is the way to know him, and live for ever with him.

Our children's publication list includes a Sunday School curriculum that covers pre-school to early teens; puzzle and activity books. We also publish personal and family devotional titles, biographies and inspirational stories that children will love.

If you are looking for quality Bible teaching for children then we have an excellent range of Bible story and age specific theological books.

From pre-school to teenage fiction, we have it covered!

Find us at our web page:
www.christianfocus.com

CF4•K
Because you're never
too young to know Jesus